MW00885751

KUNDALINI AWAKENING

AWAKEN KUNDALINI ENERGY, IMPROVE PSYCHIC ABILITIES, INTUITION, HIGHER CONSCIOUSNESS, THIRD EYE. EXPAND MIND POWER, HEAL YOUR BODY THROUGH KUNDALINI YOGA & CHAKRA MEDITATION

SERENITY MARCUS

KUNDALINI AWAKENING: Awaken Kundalini Energy, Improve Psychic Abilities, Intuition, Higher Consciousness, Third Eye. Expand Mind Power, Heal Your Body Through Kundalini Yoga & Chakra Meditation

ISBN 979-8-62998-813-7

ALSO BY SERENITY MARCUS

Spiritual Awakening: Open Third Eye & 7 Chakras Through Guided Meditation & Breathing Techniques. Develop Psychic Abilities, Empath Healing & Clairvoyance With Kundalini Awakening

Third Eye Awakening How To Awaken Your Third Eye Chakra, Increase Mind Power, Empath, Psychic Abilities, Intuition & Awareness Using Chakra Meditation & Self Healing

Psychic Empath Abilities: 2 Book In 1- The Secrets Of Highly Sensitive People To Stop Absorbing Negative Energy And Toxic Relationships. Law Of Attraction Techniques To Achieve Spiritual Awakening

Psychic Empath Abilities: The Guidebook to Help Highly Sensitive People Cast Out Stress, Negative Energy and Burnout. How to Restore Peace and Stop to Be An Emotional Sponge

Psychic Empath Abilities: Guided Meditations and Affirmation Practices To Stop Negative Spirals. Spiritual Awakening and Law of Attraction to Manifesting Your Hidden Psychic Gift

Gratitude Journal: My Daily Positivity Notebook With Self-Care Affirmations, Mindfulness And Helpful Inspirational Thoughts

Do not hesitate to contact her for any kind of practical advice on the authentic search for yourself at **serenity.marcus24@gmail.com**

Contents

PART ONE

KUNDALINI AWAKENING

AWAKEN KUNDALINI ENERGY, IMPROVE PSYCHIC ABILITIES, INTUITION, HIGHER CONSCIOUSNESS, THIRD EYE. EXPAND MIND POWER, HEAL YOUR BODY THROUGH KUNDALINI YOGA & CHAKRA MEDITATION

Introduction

The term "Kundalini" typically refers to the dimension of energy that has not realized its potential. There is an enormous well of energy inside you that is available to be tapped. This energy source is there and awaiting you to get access to it.

You are resting upon a bounty and treasure inside. Much like a hidden treasure, we need a map or blueprint to guide us and lead us to this place.

Thus if you are aware and know what the power is, you are welkun on your way to begin the journey to reaching it. The second step is to better understand what this energy can do and what you can achieve from it. Once you have completed this journey, you will be connected to an endless source of power. This is what Kundalini is.

Chapter 1: The Principles Of Kundalini Yoga

The principles on which Kundalini Yoga was built are ancient, but still very relevant in the human experience today. Again, this spiritual energy starts at the base of the spine, and the process of awakening refers to how this energy spreads from your spine to the crowd of your head with time and practice.

The metaphysical aspect of the practices describes Kundalini as an awakening snake, from which emits an energy, or chakra that takes refuge in 7 locations in the body as you grow. According to methodology, the chakra energy rises through your being in the same way that air fills your lungs then disperses oxygenated bloods throughout the vital organs of your body as you exhale.

The goal is to ascend beyond the first 6 chakras and to access the 7th through what has been called, the "golden cord". This cord, as legend has it, connects pineal and pituitary glands. The significance of this is that those glands in particular are said to have been responsible for awakening the conscious mind of a human being. And not just with

Kundalini Yoga—these glands are the subject of enlightenment in many current as well as ancient teachings. To access them is to finally see yourself and the world as it is, rather than as you think or hope it could be. The golden cord, in this particular practice, is the key to your awakening.

Kundalini Yoga combines the old teachings of three other, more specific yoga related spiritual practices. Each yoga focuses on an aspect of the human experience, from devotion (Bhakti), to power (Shakti), and mental fortitude coupled with control (Raja). Each gives an avenue on which to pursue a high consciousness, and well as to help you exploit your creative potential. It is in this way that these practices are said to be a practical technology for the conscious mind.

In addition to harnessing the power currently resting within you,

Kundalini Yoga is said to release the practicing individual from the debt of karma. If translated to western terms, being released from one's karmic debts is essentially the same as being forgiven for the mistakes that you made throughout your life. It ensures that your soul is peaceful, and that even once you physically pass on, your soul will continue to be content. It is a very interesting concept, and is yet another spiritual benefit of Kundalini Yoga.

The Health Benefits of Yoga

There is a plethora of ways in which yoga benefits the body—too many to count, in fact. So, let's explore 15 different benefits of yoga in daily life.

1. Improves flexibility – This is one of the most fundamental benefits of yoga. You may not be able to touch your toes or bend all the way forward in your first class, but you will notice over time that your body begins to loosen up, and with that will come a decrease in muscle pain as well.

2. Builds strength – Yoga is the best way to build a healthy amount of strength while balancing it with flexibility. The strength of your muscles contributes greatly to your posture, how you walk, and how you power the daily physical tasks that you may have. Lifting weights builds muscle too, but that (more often than not) takes away from your flexibility.

3. Improves posture – People underestimate the weight of their heads! When you slouch, the amount of tension of your heavy had leaning beyond your spines center of gravity can have lasting effects. Yoga encourages and promotes healthy standing and sitting positions, so you will learn over time how to sit and stand properly which will increase the longevity of your back and neck especially.

4. Stops joint/cartilage breakdown – The body is more like a machine than anything else. Like most machines, it has to be well oiled and taken care of with great compassion. Your cartilage is a spongey substance that cushions the area between your bones within joints. Yoga takes you through full ranges of motion that will loosen those joints and promote proper maintenance of your cartilage. Without going through the motions, your cartilage will likely wear with age, and eventually will be scraped down until you're experiencing the trouble and pain of two bones rubbing together

without any cartilage between them. Many elderly experience this, hence why they most so slowly. Yoga can solve this problem!

5. Spinal Protection – Spinal disks are the shock absorbers of your back, and require a healthy amount of movement to stay limber and effective. In yoga, there are many motions that involve light twisting and turning to ensure that your spine stays strong and supple through the years. Back problems affect millions of people, so it only makes sense to find a solution that can remove you from that statistic!

6. Promotes bone health – This is important for women especially! You've seen the commercials about the prescription pills that are supposed to combat osteoporosis. Well, this is a natural, much less rigorous way to prevent it. The stances and poses that you take in yoga help to strength the bones of your arms and legs especially, which is where osteoporosis likes to start. In addition to that, yoga as a whole helps to lower the amount of stress hormones produced in your body, which lowers the rate at which calcium is lost in your bones.

7. Blood flow goes up – Although yoga isn't the same as running or lifting weights, it actually is much more effective at evenly distributing oxygenated blood throughout your body. In fact, going through the motions in a session promote a higher blood flow to the areas of your body that may not always receive it as they should (hands and feet). A consistent practice will also lead to more oxygenated blood circulating healthily through your organs and tissues, and even can help with people who have had heart or kidney problems and don't get the appropriate amount of blood to certain areas of their bodies. In addition to that, this increased flow reduces your chances of unhealthy blood clots.

8. Assists immune/lymphatic system – Everything in yoga from the contraction and stretching of a muscle, to transitioning between poses allows a fluid within immune cells to break free and "drain", if you will. As it drains, your body will be able to fight off infection more readily. It also makes it so that cancerous cells are broken down faster, and also so that the toxic waste within these cells is disposed of more quickly.

9. Improves heart health – Regularly increasing your heart rate during exercise can lower your risk of heart disease as well as the chances of depression because of the endorphins released during exercise. Yoga isn't

an aerobic exercise by default, but there are variations that can be done in order to simulate a situation where your cardiovascular fitness is challenged. And even for yoga that isn't ass vigorous, it still lowers your resting heart rate and improves your overall endurance.

10. Lowers blood pressure - If you have HBP (high blood pressure), you too can benefit from yoga. The constant movement combined with the cardiovascular challenge will regulate your blood pressure, and eventually will lead to an overall drop due to the consistent practice of raising and lowering it with different forms of exercise.

11. Regulates adrenal glands – Cortisol is a stress induced hormone that appears when in a time of crisis, embarrassment, etc. Yoga reduces the amount of that this hormone sticks around. Which it first becomes present, it's helpful and makes you more alert, and even boosts your immune system. The real trouble comes when the situation that caused the increase passes and the cortisol sticks around. An overabundance of cortisol has been related to depression, osteoporosis, HBP, and insulin resistance (which can lead to diabetes). It also has been said that a constantly uninhibited influx of cortisol can lead your body to a state of crisis, and in this state the body stores most things that you may eat or drink as fat for safety purposes. Nobody wants that!

12. Improves moods – It is no secret that any form of exercise improves your overall moods, and promotes a happier existence. The consist practice of yoga will promote an increase in those "happy" hormones like serotonin and the endorphins that fill you with joy, which can be a great combatant of depression.

13. Encourages a healthy lifestyle – There is a spiritual, mental, and physical aspect of yoga. When combined, these things will trickle into other areas of your life from how to eat to how to you think act around others. Yoga encourages a heightened self-awareness, and in gaining a great appreciation for yourself, you will be more likely to begin taking better care of your wellbeing.

14. Fights diabetes – Yoga lowers your bad while increasing your good cholesterol. It makes your body more sensitive to insulin, while managing your cortisol and adrenaline levels which usually contribute to weight gain and the urge to take in more sugary foods. With a lowered blood sugar comes a lessened chance of attaining a heart disease, kidney issues, blindness, and other sugar-related diseases.

15. Improves focus – In yoga, there is no moment but the present one. The only way to master a pose is truly to focus within yourself, and to maintain that focus throughout your sessions. As your mind becomes accustomed to going to that present moment space, it will begin to show in other areas of your life as well, which can greatly improve things as small as driving to things as large as your professional career!

As you can clearly see, implementing yoga into your life would bring nothing but goodness into it. Now, imagine these health benefits coupled with what Kundalini Yoga can do for you.

Skepticism is a healthy practice, although I would not suggest it here. When it comes to the spirit, there are no gimmicks; no tricks. There is only what works, and what doesn't. This works. So, just to further prove how amazing of a practice yoga can be, I've added another 15 benefits to utilizing yoga as your physical activity for the day.

1. Relaxes your system – The relaxational aspect of yoga shifts the balance from engaging the sympathetic nervous system (fight or flight responses) to the parasympathetic nervous system (relaxation, lowered heart rates, calmness).

2. Improves balance - Proprioception refers to the ability of a person to stay aware of where their body is in space as well as how to counterbalance certain actions to keep from falling. Yoga greatly improves your proprioception, which leads to the ability to balance your body for great stents of time.

3. Maintains the nervous system – With the mastery of yoga comes a level of bodily control that many can't fathom. There are yogis in the world that can harness the usually involuntary power of their nervous system and make voluntary changes, like lowering one's

heart rate at will, or forcing blood to accumulate at a specific location in order to heal or even to incubate something (for women who want to create a healthier environment for pregnancy).

4. Releases tension – Our daily cause a lot of tension, and we don't even notice it! Everything from how you drive, to how you sit, to how you hold your face, and other subconscious actions require your muscles to operate in a certain way. Yoga will essentially help you to see where you hold tension, and in practicing you will also see it relieved over time.

5. Improves sleep experience – Along with the stimulation that comes from improved focus is the byproduct of the meditation that occurs during yoga. This byproduct of increased relaxation and decreased stress can also lead to easier, deeper sleep.

6. Improves immune cell functionality – The meditative nature of yoga increases your body's ability to respond appropriately to foreign pathogens. As needed, your body will begin to produce more antibodies and other defensive structures within the body to properly maintain homeostasis.

7. Improves lung health – Those deep breaths aren't for nothing! A constant practice of total lung expansion during yoga decreases the average amount of breaths per minute, while also increasing the level of oxygen within your blood—resulting in improved respiratory health.

8. Combats digestive trouble – Many issues of the abdominal area can be stress induced, and if they are, they can be handled by regulating your cortisol levels. As we know by now, yoga has a phenomenal effect on stress hormones. Movement promotes faster processing of foods and other materials in the body, allowing for a more regulated digestive system which can prevent constipation, colon related issues, and trouble with your digestive tract.

9. Grants peace of mind – Because of the level of inner peace attained after consistently practicing yoga, your general levels of sadness, anger, and frustration will go down. You will learn to live more in the moment, without taking things as personally or as seriously because you will learn that most of what stands before you cannot be controlled, and that your original frustration comes from attempting to control it all.

10. Increases self-confidence – Many of us deal with the burden of thinking

we aren't good enough. Yoga not only promotes the idea that you are good enough, but also that you don't need to be anything but who you are in this very moment. We live in a society of constant movement, and of chasing everything without being grateful for what you have. Yoga gives you a sense of gratitude for self, which will show in your future social interactions as confidence.

11. Assists in pain management – This can occur on a physical, mental, and spiritual level. On the physical level, yoga is great for those who experience joint pains, arthritis, and other muscle or bone related aches.

12. Grants mental fortitude – You will find that in staying dedicated to yoga, you will have gained a new level of discipline. Within this discipline lies a greater strength of mind, which most have said is the best benefit of yoga. This will translate to all other aspects of your life, and you will find that you can do more now on a social, professional, and sexual level than you ever thought you could.

13. Provides grounding – The trick to having a successful start with yoga is to find a good teacher. This teacher will essentially facilitate the beginning of your growth as a student of yoga, and will serve as a mental, physical, and spiritual guide for those who feel lost.

14. Replaces drugs with healthy habits – As you have read, you've seen now that yoga serves as a great, natural combatant to several diseases and ailments that can plague your life. Usually, each sickness comes with a list of pills that have to be taken in order to suppress or maintain them. But one thing that you must remember is that yoga is thousands of years older than modern medicine, and yet the people who lived thousands of years ago, still will able to overcome overwhelmingly more powerful illnesses! So, rather than jumping on the prescription pill train, try implementing some yoga into your daily life and see how differently you feel. The only side effect of yoga is a happier, longer life!

15. Creates greater sense of self – In gaining a greater understanding of yourself and the world that surrounds you, you will begin to be able to dissect and pinpoint where your own troubles and challenges exist within your life. It is said that rage and hostility can be just as contributory to heart problems as poor eating and physical stagnancy. So, even if you are currently experiencing something that you don't want to experience, your new level of understanding about yourself will help you to figure out what the cause of your problem is, and to do everything within your power to remedy that situation within you.

If these benefits aren't enough to prove how awesome yoga is for you and your wellbeing, I don't what to tell you! All that can truly be said is that if you really desire a greater quality of life as well as an even more powerful sense of self, this is the path for you.

Chapter 2: The History Of Kundalini

Since time immemorial, humans have been trying to understand their world and control what is in it. Artists have drawn, sang and written their interpretation of what the universe is about. Scientists have sunk a lot of time, energy and resources into research; religions have risen and fallen, all in an effort to uncover the universe's secret. Yet despite all that effort, every day something new is discovered.

However, in all these efforts most people forget to look at the most important unit of the universe themselves. You can't understand the universe, if you do not understand yourself and haven't unlocked all the innate powers that you hold within yourself. Kundalini is one of the most powerful energies of the self. Once locked it allows an individual to understand and experience their world in unimaginable ways. It allows you to exceed your spiritual, intellectual and physical limits.

The earliest mention of the word Kundalini can be traced to the Vedic writings collected. These writings were referred to as Upanishads, a word that was used to mean listening to the master's teachings while sitting down. During such lessons, the learners would be given oral recitations religious insights by a master while sitting down.

During this period, the records point out that Kundalini was an energy science and a divine philosophy. There was no physical component of the Kundalini. However, over time, the position of the Upanishads was adopted as the official physical position during yogic activities. It is still in use today. This yoga was never taught to anyone or the public. Kundalini yoga was treated as higher learning for students who had undergone rigorous preparation that would equip their bodies and their minds for the soul and body instructions from their Kundalini masters.

The choice of a follower who would be taught the science of Kundalini was done in utmost secrecy. This follower had to be from the elite family in addition to possessing particular attributes that set him apart from the rest and which were assessed by the master in secret. Once a worthy candidate was spotted, he would be initiated into the influential Indian Yoga's secret society.

Kundalini awakening was a secret kept from the public. In fact, practitioners thought they were doing the public a favor by not teaching them because; the public was not prepared to handle the power that was to be aroused in them if they knew. Such was the secrecy that covered Kundalini yoga practice.

In the Eleventh Century, the practice extended to Buddhism and Hinduism. Practitioners of these faiths began to experiment in Kundalini awakening with an aim to understanding and unleashing the immense power that lie restrained in the human body. In the Fifteenth Century, practitioners of Hatha yoga began to practice Kundalini awakening. Come the Sixteenth Century, practitioners of Upanihads Yoga began to study and practice Kundalini awakening.

For a long time after that tapping into Kundalini energy remained a preserve of the few, particularly the Chinese and Indians. They guarded it as a great secret that would only be passed from a teacher to a praiseworthy and totally loyal student. Teaching Kundalini or even making known the secret of Kundalini awakening was a taboo and attracted a severe punishment to the perpetrator of such a sin. The practice was deemed as purely religious.

Through their widely practiced yoga, they experimented with the immense power that lay restrained in the human body. These communities had a persistently rich spiritual culture that sought and still seeks to streamline and purify the human body so that it can release Kundalini that is in turn supposed to cause a transformation of the intellect. For the Chinese Taoists, to be ushered into spiritual enlightenment, also referred to as the Tao, requires that one achieve Yin Yang stability in addition to practicing the microcosmic path.

Between 1875 and 1961, Carl Jung, a psychiatrist, began a campaign to make Western countries aware of Kundalini and the immense power that comes with his awakening. Jung's efforts were largely successful because most of the West's interests in the energy can be traced back to him, as well as other practitioners.

Jung and these other practitioners had experienced Kundalini awakening and had first hand information of how the energy works. Although its manifestation was different in each of them and their interpretation of the practice of Kundalini awakening was different, they were all working from one common ground; that Kundalini was an energy sleeping in the human being that could be summoned. They also all believed that Kundalini had the ability to advance spiritual development in an individual, but needed to be controlled or mastered well.

These influential practitioners and came up with their own proposals on the practice of Kundalini awakening. One of these practitioners, George King, asserted that the entire control of Kundalini through the vertebrae is man's ultimate mission on earth. King also tried to break down the Kundalini awakening process while citing ways in which this can be achieved safely- through living a well balanced life ad devoting oneself to serving people selflessly.

Because of Jung, King and other progressives, the 60s was the decade of progression for Kundalini knowledge. No longer was it a preserve of Easterners. Many Westerners became interested in Kundalini, how to awaken it, and meditation in general. By the 1970s, Kundalini knowledge became even more popular as more people became interested in awakening their innate spiritual and intellectual powers. Driven by this need, more people were trained in awakening Kundalini the correct way as well as recognizing the signs that came with an awakening.

Currently, Kundalini has been adopted and can be mentioned alongside many religious terms or in relation to certain religious organizations, especially the newly launched ones. However, science still remains skeptical of the whole concept of Kundalini awakening, which quite frankly is no surprise since science is more focused on what can be seen, heard, touched, smelled or tasted. Kundalini is more about the sixth sense and what can be felt.

However, despite its skepticism, even science cannot ignore the increased interest in Kundalini awakening or the changes in people who have experienced it show. Currently, scientists, especially those within the medical field, have been studying Kundalini in an effort to understand how it can be applied to therapy and healing. Some medical practitioners have inculcated Kundalini yoga into their routine procedures and practice it in their clinics. A lot of research has also gone into determining the link between mental stability and meditation.

The problem with this haphazard integration of Kundalini into medical therapy is that rarely are the correct procedures for awakening followed. When this happens, side-effects to those being incorrectly prepared and awakened can be disastrous to say the least. There have been cases of patients suffering mental and emotional disturbances. Some medical personnel have therefore taken this to mean that Kundalini in general is a dangerous practice that shouldn't be tried out.

Fortunately, as the practice of Kundalini awakening grows, more and more information about Kundalini awakening is being disseminated to the public. The issue is that most of the disseminated information speaks to what the awakening is but does not go deeper into the issue explaining the step-by-step process of awakening or what to do afterwards. You're in luck because in this guide I've tried to explain these steps as well as how to do them safely.

Reality or Metaphorical Legend?

While there is no concrete proof in regards to whether Kundalini is metaphorical or absolute, the information and opinions formed are based on personal experiences. This makes proving or disproving the existence of its force difficult, at best. Individuals who are enlightened by Kundalini energy or awareness may have differing spiritual or obscure experiences. According to Hatha Yoga, the force and energy of Kundalini exists in your spine base and until stimulated (by a variety of means, exhibiting numerous sensations and responses) it hangs out in a dormant state. Yogi Bhajan expresses in his book, Kundalini, Evolution and Enlightenment, "Kundalini is the creative potential in the man".

The single, common factor among people who encounter the internal force is that each one has an awareness that gives them a deep insight into their own subtle body and soul. The subtle body is comprised of the mind, spiritual and energetic imprints, the sequence patterns, and order of energies within an individual.

Additionally, the obscure, subtle body encompasses any emotional or internal barriers.

Regardless of the opinion of medical professionals or doubt from 'non-believers', some individuals have a strong inner confidence in their belief that Kundalini does, in fact, exist. For those people who have experienced the arousal or awakening of their Kundalini energy, whether in a positive, negative, planned, or unexpected sense, they have reported feelings and sensations that are so intense that, in their minds, there is no possibility that the spiritual occurrence could be metaphorical nor imagined.

Acceptance / Non-Acceptance

Kundalini is not a medically supported phenomenon. There are no doctors who are ever going to find scientific evidence that substantiates the presence or existence of Kundalini and the energy triggered by its occurrence.

There are advocates for Kundalini who claim that a typical human being used about 1 to 2% of their brain potential, while individuals who have encountered total enlightenment through Kundalini awakening use the entire 100%.

Some medical professionals have gone as far as to say that psychotic episodes among individuals practicing yoga for the purposes of arousing Kundalini energy are just one of the connected health issues or concerns. Although there are some valid concerns in regards to adverse effects, most yoga practitioners who work with people trying to find or awaken there energy would agree that the negative incidents are most likely to occur when the individual does not follow the set instructions and take their time, trying to reach Kundalini awareness at a far too rapid pace.

Regardless of the beliefs or 'success stories' told by yoga practitioners and individuals who have experienced the effects or sensations of arousing Kundalini energy, the energy and its release are spiritual events related to the mind and soul, whereas medical professionals are seeking factual events related to the body, bones, organs, and nervous and circulatory systems.

Chapter 3: The Benefits of Kundalini

Many people assume that Kundalini awakening is for the spiritual fanatics or for people who practice Eastern religions. The truth is that everyone can experience immense benefits from awakening their Kundalini. Awakening your Kundalini is akin to activating a life force within your body; a life force that is the source of genius, creativity and psychic gifts. But what exactly does that mean in layman's terms?

Well for one, Kundalini enhances your connection with the central power you believe in. For instance, many people who pray report that it is more an automatic thing for them and that as they pray they often feel as if they are praying to empty air. However, once your Kundalini is awakened you'll feel a new spiritual connection with your God. That 'empty' feeling will no longer be there because you can actually feel your God's presence within and around you.

When you can communicate more actively with the source of your beliefs, it also makes it much easier to follow the tenets of your religion. Tasks like prayer, following commandments or rules becomes much, much easier. You'll find yourself living a much more honest lifestyle where you are honest to yourself about who you really are, your weaknesses and your strengths.

When you can be honest about who you really are then it makes accepting yourself that much easier and changing the habits you don't like about yourself much easier. Also when you accept yourself then you already know what your likes and dislikes are and who you are truly within and are therefore less likely to conform to other people's perceptions of who you are.

This honest approach to living is also better for you and the people around you. An awakening will make it easier for you to determine which people you need in your life and which relationships you need to wean yourself out of. It helps you to better appreciate the quality relationships you have and makes it easier to tend these relationships with love for a more fulfilling life.

This pragmatic approach to life extends beyond better knowledge of self and better relationships. It also makes it much easier to deal with the troubles, tribulations and unexpected occurrences of daily life. It is very unlikely to see someone who has experienced an awakening being over-emotional.

For instance, if public speaking gave you anxiety attacks before the awakening, you may find yourself suddenly calmer. There have been reported cases of people with anger problems suddenly becoming more controlled and less likely to explode. Situations like death, sickness and breakups don't seem to affect you as much. Of course, this doesn't mean you don't grieve. It means that you bounce back faster than your normally would.

An awakening will expand your awareness of your surroundings and nature around you. Taking long walks out in nature has never felt so good because you feel an almost supernatural connection with the earth and its beings. Many people have reported developing a 'green thumb' after an awakening while others say that they have a new desire to be vegetarians if only to reduce the harm they do to other creatures. You'll find yourself feeling more compassion for your fellow human being and becoming more charitable and loving.

After an awakening many people report heightened creativity. The awakening itself is akin to opening up the mind. Many people have a limited mentality that has been blocked by years of conditioning by nurture i.e. what your parents, teachers or leaders have told you. But an awakening clears away that old mentality and creates room for clarity of thought.

You may find yourself questioning every assumption you've ever made, every value you've held true, or the way you've been doing things. This is a good thing because for one you'll stop accepting everything at face value and you'll seek a better understanding of the things in your life. This process of evaluation and observation can lead to the creation of completely new and better ideas.

Many professionals have noticed that an awakening improves their work products too. Painters are able to see colors more vividly and come up with better art. Writers can write faster and better. Lawyers have better memories of laws and how to use them for their client's benefits. Regardless of profession, Kundalini awakening opens up your mind so that you are more creative and better at your job.

Kundalini awakening can also enhance your physical health and give you greater vitality. An awakening will leave your body feeling swifter and stronger. If you're trying to get in shape, exercise will suddenly feel much easier and more fun and exercise sessions will appear to fly by. Many people report increased sexual energy and libido.

If you're trying to develop better eating habits, an awakening is like cleaning up your palate so that your taste buds are more receptive to healthier, cleaner food. You'll probably find yourself developing a taste for fresh foods and vegetables and less susceptible to 'foods' that are dangerous for the body such as fatty, sugary and salty foods.

In general, an awakening will help you unlock your highest potential and thus your ultimate life. It improves your spiritual, physical and mental acuity beyond compare. You will feel healthier, look healthier and be healthier.

Can it be employed simply as a healthful practice?

The traditional yoga postures and stretches were always used to improve the flexibility of the body and to prepare for the enlightenment of the Kundalini practice, however, it can also be used to enhance the body in a healthful way. Practicing certain moves, etc. that will awaken Kundalini in an individual purely to strengthen the body appears to be an inappropriate and wasteful use of these very specific techniques.

Some trainers will guide the persons to properly practice Kundalini simply to illustrate the benefits of Kundalini on well being, without touching on its spiritual effects. In reality, these are the ways yoga was introduced in other countries for many years. And although it is commendable to try to get better and to encourage others to do so, sometimes a conflict of interest will arise between tapping any area that is meant to dissolve someone's ego and attempting to use that same energy to embrace an entirely ego-based purpose.

Chapter 4: Meditation

Meditation is strongly related to mystical experiences and Kundalini syndromes. According to a study, it is more effective than yoga and prayer in creating Kundalini syndromes. It is possible that this is because meditation involves an inner focus, which is not always involved in yoga or prayer. After all, meditation goes beyond a particular religious belief or practice, and it is something that is shared by varying cultures throughout history.

Because regular meditators experience Kundalini more often, it may mean that it is caused by the meditations or because dedicated meditators are predisposed for Kundalini experiences. No matter what the case may be, you will benefit if you regularly meditate. Not only will you train your mind to make it more capable of directing and withstanding energy, you will also receive perks like improved moods, self-control and overall health.

Mystical traditions assert that meditating upon a deity, a guru, a holy man/woman or a sacred concept will make you acquire their energetic qualities. This can mean gazing at a picture of them, chanting their name or mantra, imagining them, or emotionally connecting to them. There are certain gurus who are said to convey Shaktipat to their disciples by letting them connect to their energy via meditation.

Transcendental Meditation may activate the Kundalini – some of those who practice TM have experienced the Kundalini syndrome. This involves meditation with a mantra that may be given by the guru. An often-used mantra is "ong namo guru dev namo" which is translated to "I bow to the divine within." This connects your energy to a line of enlightened masters, ensuring that the wisdom you receive is reliable and the energy controlled.

Meditation and Multiple Practices

Based on research on meditators and Kundalini experiencers, meditation and multiple transpersonal practices increase the chances of Kundalini awakening.

It was discovered that the total amount of practice is more important than the frequency, pattern, and social conditions of practicing (de Castro, 2015). This means that it's good if you meditate a lot of times so the effect will accumulate.

Prayer

Prayer leads to mystical experiences when there are positive emotions like adoration and gratitude. When prayer involves requests or confession of sins, or if it is done out of obligation, mystical experiences occur less frequently. When praying, include in your intention that you want to be closer to God or to your idea of the Divine. You may ask that this happen specifically via Kundalini awakening, but sometimes it may occur in another form. Catholics or Christians may experience the descent of the Holy Spirit – it is similar to the Kundalini but in a form that their belief systems are already predisposed to accept.

Yoga

There are many kinds of yoga; some deal specifically with Kundalini activation. Regardless of whether yoga is done for Kundalini or not, Kundalini will more likely be awakened if yoga is practiced contemplatively. In contrast, if yoga is done mechanically and treated only as a means to attain fitness, Kundalini will remain dormant.

Yoga generally deals with physical exercises (asanas and mudras), chanting (mantras), breath control (pranayama), meditation, concentration, and visualization.

Some forms of yoga that deal with Kundalini are the following:

- Kundalini yoga/Laya yoga: Kundalini yoga incorporates Hatha yoga, Kriya yoga, visualization and meditation.
- Hatha yoga: There are particular Hatha yoga practices that are said to raise Kundalini such as mula bandha, jalandhara bandha, kechari mudra, kumbhaka, and mula bandha.
- Kriya yoga: Kriya yoga involves self-study, self- discipline, and devotions.
- Sahaja yoga: Sahaja yoga teaches Kundalini activation

methods to enable a person to achieve self-realization.

Yoga is considered as a structured path.

These Kundalini-based Yoga forms have specific techniques for activating, maintaining, and making use of Kundalini for different purposes. You can learn Yoga on your own but to be sure you carry out the techniques properly, it's best to attend a class.

Yoga improves the interconnections between the mind and body, making you more capable of directing subtle energies at will. It will make you aware of your limitations so you can surpass them. Although the postures and movements may be difficult, they will make you familiar with how your physical, mental, and energy bodies work, and eventually, you will learn how to control them so they serve you better.

Kriya Yoga

Kriya Yoga is one form of yoga that is said to be a safer alternative to forcing the Kundalini upwards. According to Paramhansa Yogananda – a yoga master from India that brought Kundalini knowledge to the West – Kriya Yoga is a technique that combines the right attitude and purity of heart with life force stimulation so that problems are avoided.

Kriyas are "activities" and can be linked to the spontaneous movements that tend to occur upon the awakening of the Shakti. The kriyas help remove the blocks that stand in the way of the kundalini as it traverses the central channel and spine. They are triggered by the energy's interaction with the blockages.

There is a belief that the higher chakras are positive magnets that pull the consciousness upwards towards the divine, while the chakra at the spine's base pulls it downwards towards ignorance, selfishness, and materialism. In this belief system, the Kundalini is the thrust of consciousness that is related to matter, and it causes the restlessness of the mind during meditation.

The goal of guiding the Kundalini upwards is to pull it away from its negative position and unite it with the positive magnet at the top of the head. The problem is, many practices just aim to shake this energy loose. However, this energy is quite dangerous, and overstimulating it causes extreme heat that may damage the person's nervous system and cause psychological disturbances.

Kriya Yoga is safer and easier than other practices, and it can also pave the way towards spiritual enlightenment. Because it's a holistic discipline, it can improve your physical and psychological well-being. Basically, it involves the cleansing of the energy channels so that energies can move more freely in the body.

These are some of the things under Kriya Yoga that can help with awakening the energy:

- Have love for the divine. This means going beyond simply practicing religious rituals just because you are taught to do them, but having a genuine desire to commune and unite with your God.
- See everything and everyone as manifestations of the Divine. The truth is, the Universe is a part of the one who created it, so you must have respect for creation as well.
- Have a positive attitude. Although life will inevitably make you feel negative at times, do your best not to get stuck in negativity. Activating Kundalini means you have to keep your energy channels clear and your frequency high.
- Do things that cause spiritual expansion. Activities that cause upliftment to yourself and others have benefits to your spiritual condition. This could be anything such as learning a productive skill, being generous to others, helping out with a cause, etc.
- Acknowledge your higher nature. All people have lower and higher natures but not all of them live as spiritual beings. The more that you are conscious of your spiritual aspect, the better your chances are of progressing spiritually.
- Develop greater awareness. Prevent yourself from going deeper into unconsciousness by indulging in things that dull your mind. Be more mindful. Participate in meaningful and productive endeavors. Try not to do things that you know are nonsensical or detrimental to you or others.

- Chanting with a devotional attitude may raise your Kundalini. Take note that inciting mantras half- heartedly may be useless.
- Be energetic. Find things to do that give you energy. Dedicate yourself to things you are passionate about. These have effects to your subtle energies as well.
- Interestingly, waking the stored Kundalini energy can be done not only by stirring it and forcing it to shoot up from below, but it can also be coaxed upward by drawing it from above. To do this, you must make your higher chakras magnetic.
- Meditating upon saints, mystics, deities, and other spiritual personas will help you with this. By calling upon them, they may help you awaken your spirituality.

Basically, the things mentioned above can help you be in touch with your spiritual nature whether you practice Kriya yoga or not. If you want to follow the path of Kriya yoga, here's a simplified version of how to do it:

Procedure

Develop and keep a good posture. Be mindful that your spine is straight for as often as you can. This will be beneficial not only to your physical health and energy level, it may also assist your Kundalini in its ascent.

Be physically active. Kriya Yoga is all about balance, so you have to balance meditation with physical exercise. Moving your body will help with removing unclean and used energy. Aerobic exercises will invigorate you and directly help with moving the Kundalini, but you may also do mild exercises such as simple stretches, head rolls, and the like.

Sit on a chair with your feet flat, or on the floor in the crossed leg or lotus position. Keep your spine straight and your head parallel to the ground. Close your eyes and remove all distractions and preoccupations from your mind.

Focus entirely on your breath. The breath is prana, so you must be sensitive to your respirations in order to work with subtle energy. Using your mind, you will direct it to bring up the Kundalini upwards through the seven chakras that line your spine.

Feel your breath stirring in the base of your spine. You may feel it becoming warmer when you do so. This is the energy becoming activated. Just accept it and bring it upwards with each breath. Be sensitive to it. Notice what it's doing. Do not force it to move but gently coax it. It will untangle coils and burn impediments on its own.

Continue bringing your breath up until you feel energy running along your spine. When you feel that the energy has reached the topmost chakra, bring your breath down one chakra at a time until you reach the heart.

Inhale from the bottom of your spine again to bring up the energy to the crown. As you exhale, bring the energy down and let it go out of your heart. This is a more balanced form of awakening; try this if you're overwhelmed by raising Kundalini from the bottom up.

Purification

Hindu tradition requires the cleansing and strengthening of the body to prepare it for the passage of Kundalini. Fasting is sometimes prescribed - this may mean not eating for a certain number of days or not eating particular kinds of food like red meat. Activities that entertain the senses are likewise prohibited to refresh the mind and make it concentrate on spirituality.

Traditionally, kundalini awakening is done in a learning setting. There are still gurus who go handpick worthy students to impart teachings that they don't share to anybody else. Nowadays, anyone who wants to learn may go to a guru or join a workshop. Kundalini Spiritual Awakening

Kundalini awakenings happen differently for everyone. For some, they are slow and come in persistently but over time. For others, it can be extremely quick, almost like an explosion of energy in the gut area. Either way, Kundalini awakenings can be quite intense for anyone who experiences them.

Here are some of the symptoms you can expect to experience during your awakening.

Remember, not everyone will experience all of the same symptoms. Furthermore, you may experience some that have not been listed here. That is okay, too. The goal is to be one with the process and welcome anything that comes your way.

Everything Seems to Fall Apart

One of the first things many people experience in the face of their awakening is feelings of nervousness. As you awaken, it may feel like everything is falling apart. This is because the world as you have come to know it is being perceived through the eyes of someone who has Kundalini that is still dormant. As a result, you may feel like everything as you know it falls away.

Many people who awaken will experience massive life changes as a result of this falling apart. Several of the aspects of their lives that are not aligned with their awakened energies will begin to drift away as they make room for new, aligned experiences in their lives. Although in the long run, this is generally all for the best, in the midst of everything falling apart you can feel intense bouts of chaos and stress. Sometimes, people will even block their awakening to lessen the chaos and prevent the stress from increasing.

Everything that has been used as a crutch to support your unhealed self will begin to render themselves as useless as you realize that they are no longer supporting you. This can, of course, be scary. Many call this "leaving their comfort zone" because they are venturing beyond the system they have carefully built around themselves to bring some peace and comfort into their lives. However, they will virtually always end up finding a more pure and true sense of comfort later in their lives when they enter a later phase of their awakening.

Physical Symptoms

Many individuals that undergo awakening experience physical symptoms as a part of the process. These symptoms are generally very random and are not linked to any health issues carried by the individual. Of course, if you do experience any ongoing physical symptoms that are particularly alarming, you should always contact your physician to rule out anything serious. However, realize that if nothing comes back and you remain "undiagnosed," it is likely that these are symptoms of your awakening.

Some of the physical symptoms people experience include anything from shaking to visual disturbances. Some will also struggle to relax as a result of the major rushes of energy that course through their bodies. Others still may even experience near-death experiences that either contributes to the awakening or are a result of the awakening. Remember, whatever symptoms you experience, if you are at all concerned you should certainly contact a physician. Even though they may be spiritual awakening symptoms, it is always important to take proper precautionary methods and look after your physical body.

The reason why many people will experience physical symptoms is that their physical body is simply unable to handle such a rush of energy. As the awakening continues, these symptoms should subside. The body will grow more accustomed to the incoming energies and will likely find it significantly easier to handle. Feeling physical symptoms may encourage you to deny your awakening, but as long as you are truly healthy, enduring them can lead to powerful results. If you are particularly concerned, you can always work alongside a Kundalini master to receive support and guidance in how to manage these symptoms and potentially slow them down to make them more manageable as you endure your awakening. In general, your physical, emotional, and energetic symptoms should last only about 20 minutes at a time.

Emotional Symptoms

Emotional symptoms are extremely common in Kundalini awakenings. In fact, they are felt by virtually everyone who experiences their awakening. Emotional symptoms vary, but early on the most common symptoms include ones like anxiety, despair, and depression. The emotions can also range in the opposite direction, bringing intense feelings of elation, joy, and an overwhelming sense of peace to the individual.

These emotional fluctuations are directly the result of the changing energy within your body. At first, they may be intense and overwhelming. You may feel as though you are encountering and enduring many mood swings, which could make it challenging to deal with. The best thing that you can do is allow yourself to embody the emotions and feel through them. Refrain from blocking them or resisting them, as this can result in you directly resisting your awakening.

Energetic Symptoms

The primary energetic symptoms experiences by individuals experiencing a Kundalini awakening are massive influxes of energies at seemingly random times. These energies can become quite powerful, resulting in people randomly feeling extremely energized and even restless. These energy symptoms are inevitable, as spiritual awakenings do exist in the non-physical life-force energy of Kundalini. You may experience many symptoms as a result. Virtually all emotional and physical symptoms stem from the energetic symptoms of your awakening.

One interesting aspect of energetic symptoms is that many will go unnoticed. Because these are less tangible than physical and emotional symptoms, many things will actually go on in the background that will contribute to your overall shift. The best thing you can do to manage energetic symptoms is to find peace, allow them to flow, and work through anything that they bring your way either physically or energetically. The more you allow them to move through, the better it will become for you.

Chapter 5: Famous Kundalini Gurus

For at least 5000 years yoga has been a crucial part of the Indian cultural and ethos system. It is ingrained in their very existence, and you would be surprised as to how yoga is practiced in India compared to in western countries. No fancy yoga mats, no fancy yoga tights- just calm and serene surroundings in whatever comfortable clothing you have and own. Did you also know that in 2014, the United Nations recognized yoga as a healthy exercise and that is 'provides a holistic approach to health and well-being'? The United Nations even concluded that yoga is beneficial for health and declared June 21 as an international day of yoga.

1. *Tirumalai Krishnamacharya*

Tirumalai Krishnamacharya Is credited as being the father of modern yoga. he is the architect of vinyasa, and he is also credited with the Revival and practice of Hatha Yoga. He is mainly known as a healer and has immense knowledge in both yoga and Ayurveda to restore one's health. Ayurveda is the ancient Indian medicine approach using herbs and natural ingredients.

Tirumalai toured around India under the patronage of the Maharaja of Mysore to promote yoga. He is known to have control over his heartbeat and is also believed to have mastered holding heartbeats as well.

2. Swami Sivananda

According to yoga tradition, the number one trait that a Yogi must possess is humor. This is one of the biggest traits that this Swami advocates. Swami Sivananda was by profession a doctor. Swami Sivananda penned a poem describing the properties that a Yogi should have and should practice, and humor was the number one trait. He is famous for teaching yoga of Trinity or known as Trimurti yoga. Trimurti yoga is a combination of karma yoga hatha yoga and master yoga.

3. B K S Iyengar

He is one of the earliest students of T Krishnamacharya. He is known to have popularized yoga internationally and to the Western world. Since his childhood, BKS Iyengar has been struggling with diseases which left him very weak. Yoga was the one thing that made him stronger which is why he redefined the Patanjali Yoga sutras to what we now know as Iyengar yoga. BKS Iyengar died at the ripe old age of 95, and it was his yoga regimen that kept him fit despite suffering 2 heart attacks, one in 1996 and the other one in 1998. He has over a million followers in over 70 countries. His book published in 1966 and entitled light of yoga is considered the Bible for yogis and over 3 million copies have been sold and translated into 19 languages.

4. K Pattabhi Jois

K. Pattabhi Jois was popular among many of Hollywood's elite. Pattabhi Jois was popular for Ashtanga Vinyasa yoga or popularly known as ashtanga yoga. Celebrities such as Sting, Madonna, and Gwyneth Paltrow were fans of his yoga.

5. Maharishi Mahesh Yogi

This famous yogi pioneered the meditation technique called transcendental meditation. The Beatles were among the famous followers of this technique. This technique is performed entirely with eyes closed.

6. Jaggi Vasudev

This Yogi is also known or popularly called s this Yogi is also known or popularly called sadhguru. He is a Philanthropist from Karnataka India. He founded Isha foundation. This foundation offers yoga programs throughout the world. One of the primary focuses of this Guru is that he focuses on yoga programs for long-term

Prisoners and those who are incarcerated for life. He has also done a yoga session with the Indian hockey team in 1996.

7. Paramahansa Yogananda

This Yogi is responsible for bringing yogurt to the west apart from the ever-famous Yogi Bhajan. He introduced the teachings of meditation and Kriya yoga to the west. This form of yoga focuses on uniting the infinite concepts through a series of Kriya.

8. Sri Sri Ravi Shankar

He is popularly known as the founder of the art of living foundation. Through him, the rhythm of breathing practices was popularized. This Breathing practice is called Sudarshan Kriya. He has said that this breathing practice came to him like a poem. He came up with this with him as he was silently practicing for a 10-day long period by the banks of the Bhadra River, in Karnataka.

9. Baba Ramdev

Baba Ramdev is more popular you know now for black money issues. He is more commonly seen in the political cycle rather than in yoga cams these days. Despite his issues, it was his best yoga camps that brought yoga back to popularity.

Though today, he is seen more in the political circle he started the practice of yoga programs which was shown on TV, and this became such a huge hit and made him a household name in India. This man is also responsible for popularizing Kapalbhati and Anulom-vilom meditation techniques. He made practitioners believe and understand that yoga is for everyone and just not yogis.

10. Bikram Choudhury

This list would not be complete without mentioning Bikram Chowdhury. He brought to the world the famous 26 types of posture meant to be practiced in an environment of 40°C. These postures are taken from hatha yoga, and it is designed specifically to bring the body back to the brain. Each of the 26 poses benefits a chakra or part in our body. If anyone talks to you about yoga in a hot environment then it is definitely Bikram yoga.

Chapter 6: The 4 Elements

A discussion on the 4 elements

There are four elements: fire, water, air, and earth. Everything in creation is composed of the elements. Take note that these elements do not refer to their gross material significance. Hence, the element fire does not just refer to the physical fire, as you know it. Rather, it refers to certain qualities. Each element has its own qualities or characteristics. Let us discuss them one by one:

- *Fire*

Fire is said to be the very first element in the universe. It has the following qualities: expansion, courage, lust, willpower, motivation, love, sexuality, authority, and passion. Fire is associated with the sun; hence, its day is Sunday. Its season is summer, and the part of the body associated with it is the head. If left unbalanced, fire can be destructive. It can control your emotions and even make you do things that you would not want to do if only you were in control of it. Fire is powerful, and it can hurt even the one who wields it.

- *Water*

Water is like the opposite of fire. It has the following qualities: magnetic, cleansing, psychic powers, cool and moist, healing, and beauty. It is considered to have a feminine nature. Its color is blue, and its elemental spirits are the undines. This element also rules autumn and sunsets. Its elemental tool is the chalice. If you want to cleanse and heal, then you would want to work with the water element.

- Air

The element, air, has the following qualities and attributes: intellect, communication, mental power, abstract thinking, divination, teaching, freedom, laughter, visualization, and astral travel, among others. Its direction is the east. It is hot and moist. The elemental being of the element air is the sylphs. Animals associated with this element are those that have wings and fly, such as butterflies and eagles. Its elemental color is yellow.

- Earth

This element has the following qualities and attributes: stability, grounding, nature, money, prosperity, crops, home, wealth, protection, and animals, among others. It is dry and cold. Its elemental color is brown and green. Its elemental beings are the gnomes. It is worth noting that humans have been swimming in the earth's energy. There is simply no escape from it.

Akasha

Everything in the universe is said to be composed of the four elements. These four elements came from what others refer to as the fifth element: akasha. However, it should be noted that akasha is not really an element. It is where all the elements originate. Hence, there are people who think of akasha as God. Another term for akasha is spirit. Its color is white and black, and it governs everything, as being the source of everything in creation. In fact, through the invocation of akasha, all psychic abilities can be developed.

Application

Now that you know the qualities of the elements, you can now use them to your advantage. The way to do it is to incorporate them in your visualization. For example, if you need healing, then visualize bathing in the element of water. Allow it to heal you completely. If you want to draw more courage, then you can visualize inhaling the element of fire. You can device other techniques according to your need and preference. The key is to take in the element, using visualization, and allow it to manifest through you.

The ancient alchemists also divided the human body in accordance with the four elements:

Head – Fire Chest
– Air Stomach –
Water
From the waist and down – Earth

It is believed that you can bring the body into harmony by charging it with the correct elements. The steps are as follows:

Assume a meditative position. Relax. Now, imagine your head being filled with the element of fire. Next, visualize the chest region being filled with the element air. Next, visualize your stomach filled with water, and then from the waist down, with the earth element. Visualize and feel all the elements in their right positions all at once. By the time you reach this point, you will be in a trance state. Enjoy the moment and feel your whole body in complete harmony with the elements of the universe. When you are ready to end the meditation, simply think of your physical body, move your fingers and toes, and slowly open your eyes.

Indeed, mastery of the elements can open up manifold opportunities. It only takes a bit of the imagination to realize the great power you can possess by working on the elements.

Chapter 7: How Is Kundalini Yoga Different From Other Types Of Yoga?

The Basics of Kundalini Yoga

This type of yoga is an ancient science and art which deals directly with the expansion and transformation of consciousness. The end result after dedicated practice is the raising of Kundalini energy, which flows through the chakras. Through the combination of pranayama, bandhas, asanas, mudras, and mantras, there is a build- up pressure, which forces the Kundalini energy to be awakened to rise up through the body. In addition to these exercises, focused attention, projection, and visualization are key to acquiring specific effects.

When a person practices Kundalini Yoga, they are able to unite their consciousness with the Ultimate Consciousness when they practice on a daily basis. It is not a quick process, and much care needs to be taken to ensure that specific combinations of exercises are performed. Once a student starts to perceive the movement of energy outside, and within the body, they are able to consciously direct the flow of the pranic energy to unblock, clear, and awaken the chakras. In turn, they will be healing themselves and even others as they become one with the universal energies.

Kundalini yoga has been gaining popularity since the 1980s in the West since Yogi Bhajan brought over the teachings from India. He was considered a Kundalini master at the young age of 16. He first emigrated to Canada in 1968 and shortly thereafter moved to Los Angeles, California to teach Kundalini. His utmost goal was to make each individual holy, happy, and healthy. His non-profit organization named 3HO is still functioning today through his students as he passed away in 2004.

The typical traditional Kundalini yoga sessions include a balanced distribution of physical yoga poses, meditation, and breathing exercises. They also incorporate mantras into their meditations, which assist the newcomer in mediation with the silence, which is required for meditation.

These mantras differ from other Sanskrit mantras which are commonly used in Sanskrit because they are usually from the Gurmukhi language.

The combination of different aspects of yoga practice is known as kriya, which translates to "action" from Sanskrit. A particular kriya will have a focus such as a physical, emotional, or mental health benefit. These can range from letting go of anger, discovering inner intuition, or eliminating health issues such as lower back pain or poor digestion. Some of the names of these kriyas are Kriya for Conquering Sleep, Navel Adjustment Kriya and Kriya for Elevation.

Hatha Yoga

Known as the most popular form of yoga in the West, Hatha yoga is focused more on the physical practice of yoga compared to Kundalini. However, the physical practices were taken from Hatha yoga to be practiced in Kundalini yoga. People who practice Hatha yoga do not perform the mantras and pranayamas into their exercises.

Hatha yoga was born out of Tantric yoga practices and is believed to be approximately 5,000 years old. The first text which was written about Hatha yoga was written by Swami Swatamarama in the 15th century. The core belief of Hatha is that enlightenment could be attained when you strengthened the connection with your physical Self.

The traditional practice of Hatha consists of some breath work or a short meditation in which they proceed with many different yoga poses. Some of the poses which are common to Hatha yoga are Warrior, Mountain, Child's, and Downward Dog pose. As the individual is practicing the yoga poses, it is a slow process that is marked by precision and striving to make the pose correct and perfect. It is not necessarily a fast-paced or physically demanding type of yoga; however, there are always exceptions.

In respect to Kundalini yoga, Hatha yoga share several of the same physical positions and breathing exercises. Sometimes a Hatha practitioner may even use some of the mantras which are used in Kundalini yoga. The largest difference between the two is how the yoga sessions are structured with Hatha yoga focusing on bettering the physical Self and Kundalini yoga's focus is on the spiritual experience, which can be felt inwardly. However, both types of yoga strive to increase awareness and flexibility, remove stress, and have a goal of becoming balanced in body, mind, and spirit.

Bhakti Yoga

This style of yoga is understood to be the path to a devotion, which is based on emotion and reality based on our emotions. Emotions are the root of the most intense experiences we have in our reality. Feelings are able to make us experience the highest highs and the lowest hells. They can unite people together for their lifetime or burn bridges without the thought of looking back. Certainly, everyone can agree that emotions are the number one intense experience that we can have as human beings.

The purpose of bhakti yoga is to teach a way to control these intensely emotional experiences so that they can live their life for the better.

The devotional path of bhakti teaches their students how to transform their negative emotions into more pleasing ones. The way they view life is through eyes of love. When you focus your mind on love and how it makes you feel, it can make everything in your life look that much brighter. It also plays on the Law of Attraction.

Being in a state of love also has a chemical effect on the brain. There is more dopamine released into the brain when you are feeling love or remembering memories that are close to your heart. When you feel this way, you tend to ignore or forget about all the negative things in your life and around you.

Some people may think this is too much of an unrealistic way of viewing life. However, it is very detrimental to be bogged down with negative emotions of anxiety, anger, sadness, or stress. There needs to be a happy medium. However, bhakti yoga only focuses on this one aspect, whereas Kundalini yoga is much more profound on an internal and external level.

Gnana Yoga

For those who want to strengthen their intellect and mind, jnana yoga is right up their alley. However, this is not necessarily for the Harvard graduate. How we define intelligence in today's society, it is very ego-based and materialistic. True intelligence cannot be measured by test scores, complex thoughts, or big words. No, the real type of intelligence is not attached to a value or a particular outcome.

This type of intelligence is gathered in a particular way because of your awareness level of activities occurring around you. It brings about complete focus without getting wholly involved. You could say that the motto of jnana yoga is "it is what it is" as they embrace this fact. It is a form of detachments as intellect disbelieves nothing and simultaneously believes in nothing.

Karma Yoga

There is a misunderstanding that there is good and bad karma. However, the truth of the matter is there is simply karma. The definition of karma is the use of the physical energy within your body. The belief in karma yoga is that there is a coiled spring located inside of each of us which much be released during physical activity. If this spring is not released, there will be a buildup of energy with us which will need to be released. When this becomes the case, it causes people to become nervous and agitated.

During karma yoga, the eternal actions which are performed are expending the karma which is centered around this coiled spring. When energy is dispersed each day, it can be a liberating experience rather than entangling. The activities that are performed are not necessarily things that you want to do, but because they need to be done.

The end result of this activity is that it causes a stillness within you that becomes your reality. It is not just an idea because it becomes your life.

Kriya Yoga

This type of yoga focuses on the emotions, mind, and body being external to you as they are not what defines you. Instead, they are your realities based on your experiences in life. Kriya in this sense if your energy which is a reality experienced internally.

The motto which could be used for this type of yoga is that "everything happens for a reason," and it is not part of the practice to come to the bottom of the reasoning. However, the purpose of kriya yoga is to put trust in the process and open yourself up to the possibility that nothing can have an explanation in the physical world. The reasoning for this thought is that the ego tries to explain everything as it assigns, meaning the insignificance and chaos of our individual lives.

They believe they are just energy which the use of a body and mind which helps to facilitate their experiences in this life. They are able to separate their physical experience of living from their energy. They want to understand the inner workings of the energy and soul within them.

Of course, when it comes to Kundalini yoga, all these types of yoga are just smaller pieces to a larger puzzle. Kundalini digs deeper than any of the other types of yoga. It also much more physical and requires a great deal of dedication if you want to realize the true end goal of Kundalini - to have the coiled serpent rise through all of your chakras. The end result is the liberation and freedom from the confines of this bodily existence. It is surreal and unimaginable and quiet difficult to attain without guidance. However, there are steps that anyone can take to start on the path to enlightenment.

In short, all other types of yoga focus on one central point within ourselves. Kundalini yoga makes you take apart each part of yourself to examine and polish or toss away parts of ourselves that do not mesh truly with who you are inside. There is simply no comparison. As long as you come to this path of yoga with sincerity and respect without expecting to experience actual awakening after doing it for a few months, then you are prepared to start.

Kundalini Yoga Asanas & Mudras

All of the poses listed are recommended to use during Kundalini Awakening as well as clearing out the chakras to prepare for the Kundalini energy to rise.

Adho Mukha Svanasana - Downward-Facing Dog Pose (Variation)

- Position your hands and knees on your mat. Place your knees straight below your hips.

- Set your hands together with your only thumbs touching and angle your fingers slightly angled outwards.

- Exhale as you lift your knees while keeping them slightly bent and the heels just above your mat.

- Stretch your spine and press lightly towards the pubic bone. This will take the stress off your shoulders.

- Contract the outer arms and press against the base of your index fingers.

- Your head should be kept steady between your arms and not drooped down.

- Take long and deep breaths for 3 minutes as the prana is allowed to flow towards your brain.

Benefits of Adho Mukha Svanasana

- Strengthens the feet, shoulders, legs, and arms
- Relieves fatigue, insomnia, headache and calms the mind
- Aids in healthy weight loss
- Lengthens the spine and increases lung capacity
- Energies and rejuvenates the body
- Treats the symptoms of sciatica as well as lung disorders such as asthma
- Eliminates menstrual discomfort pain
- Improves digestion and eliminates constipation
- Treats sinusitis and other allergy symptoms

- Strengthens the bones and prevents osteoporosis
- Relieves the symptoms of menopause

Bakasana Crow Pose

- Stand on top of your mat with your arms loosely at your sides. Keep your feet at the edges of the mat.
- Bend your knees and lower your hips as you come down to the position of a squat. Kccp an cqual amount of wcight on both of your feet.
- Keep the thighs set slightly wider than the shoulders.
- Lower your chest slightly and place the upper arms at the inside of the knees.
- Keep your spine straight as possible while slightly pressing inwards at the pelvic bone.
- Hold this pose for half a minute up to 3 minutes before proceeding.
- Place your palms flat on the mat about shoulder-width apart and spread your fingers.
- Hold your shins against the back of your upper arms. Make sure to keep the knees as near to the underarms as you are able.
- Round out your back and contract the muscles in the abdomen. The tailbone should be tucked in towards your heels.
- Focus on the area of the mat between your hands.
- As you continue to lean forward, lift your feet off of the floor, and push your heels towards your buttocks.

o If lifting both of your feet is too difficult at first, try lifting one foot at a time.

- Balance your legs and chest on the back of your upper arms.

• Be sure to have even pressure throughout your fingers and palms as you straighten the elbows.

• Keep the shins and knees touching the armpits and keep your forearms touching your core.

• Press your navel towards your spine as you touch your big toes together while keeping your breath steady and smooth.

• Exhale and slowly lower your feet to the mat. Stay in the squatted position with your feet slightly wider than shoulder length apart.

• Form the Anjali mudra again and press your elbows once again to the insides of the knees.

• When complete, lay down on your mat either in a lotus position or in savasana to notice the effect of the exercise.

• Return your breath to a normal rate.

• Pay special attention to the physical area of the perineum, tailbone, and hips.

Benefits of Bakasana

• Increases physical and mental strength

• Allows the body to be more flexible

• Strengthens the shoulders, wrists, abdominal and forearm muscles

• Cleans and energizes the sacral chakra

Bhekasana - Frog Pose

• On your mat, place your heels together as you place your fingers on the mat in front of you.

• Inhale through your nose as you straighten your knees.

• As you exhale again through your nose, bend down to a squat position.

Benefits of Siddhasana

- Stabilizes the nervous system and reduces symptoms of anxiety and mental frustration
- Aids the practitioner to control sexual functions and sexual urges
- Helps the Kundalini energy to move upwards as the heel is pressed into the perineum.
- Prepares the body for meditation

Sukasana - Easy Pose

- Sit on your mat with your legs crossed at the ankles.
- Press the lower spine slightly forward so that the back is erect.
- You can also perform this pose sitting in a chair with your feet both planted firmly on the floor.

Benefits of Sukhasana

- Stretches the back, neck and spinal cord
- Reduces fatigue and lack of energy
- Helps the joints of the hips, knees, and ankles to be more flexible
- Balances out the mind and body so you feel calmer
- Strengthens the back muscles while improving your posture
- Expands the collarbone and chest

Supta Utthita Tadasana - Stretch Pose

- Lay down flat on your mat with your arms lying next to your sides.
- Simultaneously lift the feet and the head up to 6 inches off of the mat.
- Lift the arms still outstretched with the palms facing the mat.
- Fix your gaze upon your toes.

Benefits of Supta Utthita Tadasana

- Improves circulation, respiration, and posture
- Heightens concentration and focus
- Opens the practitioner to feelings of happiness and love
- Enhances emotional balance
- Aligns the chakras
- Particularly balances and charges the heart chakra

Swastikasana - Auspicious Pose

- Sit on your mat with your legs lengthen out in front of you.
- Set your hands on the mat next to your hips with your palms touching the mat and your fingers facing forward.
- Shake the legs a few times to relax the muscles.
- Bend your left knee and set the sole against the inside of your right thigh and your heel against your perineum.
- Hold on to your right foot by using your right hand to hold the front of your ankle and use your left hand to grip your big toe.
- Place your right foot in between your calf and thigh so that only your

big toe is showing.

- Place your hands on your knees with your palms facing down and your arms relaxed.

- Stretch your spine and neck so that they are erect.

Benefits of Swastikasana

- It is a good position for those who are not able to perform the asanas of Padmasana and Siddhasana.

- It is a good position for those who have leg pains or varicose veins

- Promotes calmness of mind

- A good position for concentration during meditation

Ustrasana - Camel Pose

- Kneel on your mat and place your thighs and hips at a 90-degree angle to the floor.

- Keep the muscles of the shins loose as your press the top of your feet firmly into your mat.

- Move your thighs inwards and bend backward.

- Touch the soles of your feet with the palms of your hands.

- Be sure that your face is upward towards the ceiling as you arch your back.

- Press your shoulder blade inwards to allow your chest and heart chakra to be more open.

- Relax the muscles of your throat while you audibly hum on your exhales.

- Hold this pose for up to three minutes while deeply breathing.

• When the pose is complete, breathe deeply and fill the lungs. Hold your breath for a few seconds.

• During your exhale, slowly lift your head as you lower your hips gradually so that you are sitting in rock pose on top of your heels.

• Allow your breathing to come back to normal and contemplate the effects of the asana.

• If this stretch is too much when you start to practice, place your hands on the small of your back rather than your feet as you arch your head.

Benefits of Ustrasana

• Clears and balances the chakras

• Activates the thyroid glands

• Improves and stimulates the nervous and respiratory systems

• Stimulates the digestive system, kidneys, and endocrine glands

• Reduces fatigue and anxiety as it energies the body

• Strengths the back, thighs, arm and shoulder muscles

• Loosens the spinal cord, improves posture and opens up the hips

• Stretches the hip flexors, quadriceps, abdomen, and chest.

Vajrasana - Rock Pose

• On your mat, sit on top of the heels of your feet like the top of your feet are lying flat on the mat.

• Stretch your spine and neck so that they are erect.

Benefits of Vajrasana

- Aids in proper digestion and liver function
- Relieves symptoms of indigestion, constipation, nerve issues, and sciatica
- Balances out the acidity in the stomach and prevents ulcers
- Strengthens the pelvic and back muscles
- Reduces menstrual cramps and eases labor pain
- Prepares the body for meditation

Benefits of Vajrasana

- Aids in proper digestion and liver function
- Relieves symptoms of indigestion, constipation, nerve issues, and sciatica
- Balances out the acidity in the stomach and prevents ulcers
- Strengthens the pelvic and back muscles
- Reduces menstrual cramps and eases labor pain
- Prepares the body for meditation

Savasana - Corpse Pose

- Lay on your back on your mat and bend your knees slightly.
- Keep your arms straight at your sides.
- Center your head while facing straight at the ceiling.
- Extend both of your hands to the sides parallel to the body.
- Breathe normally, and let the air flow smoothly.

- Close your eyes and relax the facial muscles starting with the eyelids and forehead.

- Secondly, relax your tongue, lips, and cheeks.

- Continue to relax all the muscles in your body methodically going in section towards your feet.

Chapter 8: Prana

What is Prana?

It is called by many names and terms, yet they all refer to the same divine energy: prana. Even some people claim so far that since prana is everywhere and that it cannot be destroyed, then perhaps prana is God. There are conflicting schools of thought on this matter, but the majority believes that prana only comes from God, but it is not God. Still, the nature of prana remains the same: It is everywhere; it is infinite; it cannot be destroyed but is transmuted from one state into another; and that everything – both visible and invisible – is made of prana. Without prana, then there is no life. From this perspective, it is not hard to say that perhaps prana, indeed, is God. However, this is something that you may have to decide on your own.

Understanding the Nature of Prana

Prana is said to be everywhere. It is inside you and all around you. No life can exist without prana. Prana is also in the breath. Hence, there is a famous practice known as pranayama, which is a practice of controlling one's prana by controlling the breath. Another nature of prana is that it cannot be killed or destroyed. Instead, it can only change or be transmuted from one state into another. It is interesting to note, that conventional science has also proven this teaching, that energy cannot be destroyed; it only changes.

Everything in the universe swims in an ocean of energy. Perhaps this is also how everything is said to be connected. Hence, the web of life.

Prana or energy can also be used for various purposes. It is not just for awakening the Kundalini. Many people use it for healing, such as in reiki and in pranic healing. It can also be used for many other purposes, even for evil. Indeed, prana is everything and everything is composed of prana. Although prana may be seen as one and the same, it should be noted that its quality might vary. When you use prana, only focus on harnessing positive energy.

There are many other ways to direct prana, although the simplest and usual way of doing it is by visualization.

Other known ways include dancing, chanting, and certain movements, among others.

Prana is considered important to humans. People with low prana are often more prone to getting sick, while people with lots of prana are more likely to be active and healthy.

Prana or chi has been in existence for centuries; in fact, ancient writings also talked about prana. Mind you, these writings can be traced back to before the time of Christ. However, although prana has been known and used for so long, it is not yet accepted by conventional science. Still, this does not mean that it is not real. Just because science cannot explain something does not mean that it does not exist.

Chapter 9: The Source, Akasha

Akasha or the source. It is believed to be the fifth element in which the four other elements originate from. It is the origin of all things. There are some people who view Akasha to be the god principle. While it isn't technically an element, meaning you can't physically create it, it does possess all elements. It is most closely associated with the colors black and white. It does not conform to space or time. It is infinite. It is the beginning and the end. It's easy to see why many people associated Akasha with God. They are both described in similar manners, so it is perfectly fine to view Akasha as God if it helps.

Since Akasha possesses all of the qualities of the elements and holds all colors, mastering Akasha will give you the power to master the elements. This is by no means as simple as it may sound. To master this power requires a very high level of spiritual development and maturity. Still, it is something that can be done while you continue along your spiritual quest.

Just like the elements, everything in the Universe that can and cannot be seen comes from Akasha. Nothing is able to escape the power of Akasha because it is everywhere.

Some even believe that Akasha holds the records of everything that has happened or will ever happen of the past, present, and future. With a developed clairvoyant ability, a person can tap into the records of the Akasha and share somebody's future. This is the method that many psychics and diviners use.

Akasha lives within the astral plane. This is the reason for the spaceless and timeless ability of the astral plane. It's also important to know that every physical being has an astral counterpart. In fact, everything exists in the astral plane before they are given a physical body. Every plane is the same. They only differ in the types of vibrations that live within them. It's easy to understand that Akasha has the highest vibration of all the elements.

You do not have to master Askasha to benefit from its power. Mastery can end up taking years or your entire life to achieve, so it's important to start using its benefits now. When you start to work with Akasha, you will start to notice improvements in your psychic abilities, your chakras, and your energy overall.

There are some practitioners who do nothing but try to master the power of Akasha since it is the key to all things. However, gaining psychic powers and the like should not be your reasoning behind your spiritual focus. Gaining these powers is just a byproduct of awakening your Kundalini energy. You should focus on gaining spiritual maturity and not be blinded by gaining power.

Akasha is also sometimes referred to as intelligence. Whether or not this intelligence will help you or hinder you will determine your life; whether you become blessed or are someone who gets knocked around by life. Both types of people can easily be seen in life. There are some that seem to get everything they ever wanted and others who work their butt off but get nowhere. It is that person's ability, either unconsciously or consciously, to allow this power to influence their life.

A common practice that can be done to help Akasha work for you is to get up each morning before the sun rises and as the sun comes up, and before it passes at an angle of 30 degrees, look up to the sun and bow down to Akasha, thanking it for keeping you where you need to be. At another point during the day, anytime, look at the sky and bow again. Once the sun has set, look up at the sky and bow again. This isn't being done to a god or anything. This is being done for the empty space that has held you in place. You will be amazed how your life will change when you do this.

Without Akasha, just like without prana or air, you can't exist. It's easy to understand that without air you can't live. You need air to breathe. The vast majority of people don't even acknowledge the air around them, yet they are constantly using it. It can't be seen, but we know it's there. That is how Akasha works. We can't see it or touch it, but it is there and it is necessary for our survival.

In southern India, in the town of Karnataka, there is a temple dedicated to Annapoorneshwari. At the back of the temple, an inscription is written in Hale Kannada that describes how to design an airplane. It talks about how it should be constructed and it talks about how when the machine is flown, it will disrupt the ether. They believed that if the Akasha is disturbed, humans wouldn't be able to live peacefully. When Akasha is disturbed, psychological disturbances will become prevalent. This disruption has happened and we must live with it, but we can still use Akasha and actively work to improve ourselves with its power.

A person can access their own Akashic records without a lot of training or practice because they are their own. This is very different from accessing somebody else's, which takes a lot more practice and spiritual maturity. They can be accessed from anywhere and at any time. There are some directions that you should make sure you follow. When you do decide to connect with your own records, what is best for you will show itself. You don't have to have advanced psychic abilities to access your own records. All you need to be is alive and have a true heartfelt desire to get started. Lastly, you have to believe in yourself.

Accessing the Akashic records isn't something that only a few people are allowed to do, and as long as you have a pure heart, it won't be that difficult. Anybody can do it in many different ways. What plays the biggest part in this is the motivation behind it. If a person attempts to access the records out of mere curiosity, not to mention malicious intent, they will be misinformed or rejected. Curiosity comes through in many different innocent ways, like, "Let's see what my spouse was in a past life..." Accessing their records and learning about their past lives isn't going to help your relationship until you have come to understand who you are. You want to start with yourself.

I'm going to provide you with a quick practice to access your own records. Accessing your own is easier because you carry yours with you, so to speak. This means you don't have to access the hall of records that live within the astral plane. While it may not be difficult to access your own records, there are a few prerequisites. The first is being able to get into a meditative state. You have to know how to place your current thoughts to the side and be open to the information that you may receive.

Secondly, you must be willing to accept and reveal whatever is in your records. You can receive disturbing information from past lives and the like, so you have to make sure you are in a place where those things can be accepted. If you tend to avoid problems or steer clear of challenges in your daily life, how are you going to face this type of information in your records?

It's also a good idea to have a compassionate understanding of humanity so that your reading is meaningful. For example, you could learn that you were a slave owner in a past life. For most, this will be seen as a horrible thing, but that thought will close your heart and cause the reading to stop. Just because you were a slave owner doesn't mean you were a cruel person. You could have treated them fairly and kindly, but it was the norm for those times and you had very few options available to you. Having not moved past this past life could be what is affecting your current life. That's why it's important that you go into your readings understanding that past lives happen the way they do because of those times. The more understanding you have of life, the better your readings will be.

Having a bit of a ritual before your reading is always a good idea. Some preparatory meditation is great. It's also a good idea to voice your intention. Saying something along the lines of: "Allow the energy of truth and love to live on Earth. I would like my spirit guides to help me access my Akashic records so that I can have the wisdom to live my life with courage and awareness." Saying something with the words love, truth, and light will make it clear that you are doing this with love and without judgment. Truth lets the Universe know that you don't want to be given false information and that you are open to the truth no matter what it is.

It's very important that you have a reason for doing this and not just "let's see what I get" kind of attitude. You could end up receiving a lot of information that may not be influential to your current life. You want to be as clear and direct as possible.

To start, ask something along the lines of, "This (briefly describe your problem) is what I have been trying to work on, and I think there is more to it than what I know presently. If this is true, please send me information on how and when this problem started."

The way you get your answer will depend on your psychic strength. You could receive a video clip or picture on your vision screen. You could hear a clip of music that means something. You could taste, smell, or feel something. Or, you could just realize that you know something. It could also be a combination. Allow this information to come in and then ask a few clarifying questions if you need to. Once you are done, close the session with gratitude. You were given what you need to know in that moment.

You will want to have a journal and write down the things you learn immediately so that you don't forget anything. As far as knowing if it is accurate, you will just know. It will make sense to you. Sometimes people will experience changes, have pains disappear, and some experience a

cold before they become better. These don't happen all the time or to everybody.
There may be times when the reading doesn't resonate with you, but it is still accurate. This is when you have received a reading has revealed an uncomfortable truth. Don't allow yourself to fall into denial. These readings can lead to big changes.
When you first do this, keep your readings brief. There is a lot of information in your records, so you must keep yourself focused. You don't want to end up overwhelmed. This can cause inaccuracy.
I also must caution you this, once you get used to access your own records, you could be tempted to access other peoples'. You should not do this EVER unless you have their explicit consent. Reading another person's records without their consent is like breaking into their house and stealing personal information. No matter how benevolent your reasoning may be, it's still wrong. Now, you can read family members' records without consent to the extent of what is relevant to you.
The most important thing is to make sure that you treat these records with respect because Akasha knows everything.

Chapter 10: Kundalini And The Chakras

Kundalini Awakening is directly linked to the concept of chakras, or nadis in the body. You may have already heard of them or seen pictures in yoga studios, or online, of what they look like in relation to the human body.

You could also see each as a swirling vortex. These wheels are the main energy centers of your body, or rather your "subtle-body" as it is often termed in yogic texts.

Each chakra also has qualities, similar to how you might describe human qualities. For example, the 4th chakra, or heart chakra lies where your heart is in your chest. If you were going to describe this chakra to someone, you might say that it is loving, open, generous and warm. You might also say that it is overly protective, defensive, and afraid to give and receive love. When the heart chakra is balanced and open, the energy of this chakra allows for the generosity of love. If blocked or congested, the heart chakra can create closed energy which prevents the flow of giving and receiving love and affection.

Since each chakra has its own qualities, colors, and vibrations, they may seem to be individual, but one doesn't function well without the others also flowing well. Sometimes, due to life experiences, physical or emotional trauma, diet, habits, and other factors, chakras can become imbalanced where they are either excessive (too much) or diminished (not enough). Additionally, a chakra can become blocked which means there is a lack of flow, causing stagnation. These stagnations can, over time, lead to illness, disease, chronic health conditions, and mental health issues.

Along with its qualities, color, and vibrational quality, each chakra is also associated with specific organ systems in the body including glands, sex organs, digestive organs, body parts, etc.

That is where Kundalini Awakening plays a big part. The object of awakening is to adjust and balance the chakras and to eliminate the excesses, deficiencies or blockages that impede healthy, happy living and spiritual enlightenment. Understanding each chakra and what part they play in your own alignment process is significant and important. It will help the ascension process flow more smoothly if you can identify any of these blockages or imbalances.

In the following pages, you will learn about each chakra and how they may be affected by the Kundalini awakening process. You may already have an idea about what feels out of alignment for you. As read, take into account which chakras jump out at you and resonate with how you are feeling right now in your life. Notice, too, as you read if any of them resonated with past experiences. Use your intuition (more on that later) to consider and feel your energy while you are reading about each chakra. Even take some notes about feelings that come up as you are reading.

Chapter 11: Kundalini And 7 Main Chakras

The base chakra is the beginning of the energetic journey in the subtle body. Its Sanskrit name means "root". It is the Earth element. It is survival. It is the right "To Have". It is here that the Kundalini energy is stored. This is the place of physical health, grounded-ness, stability, youthful quality, vitality, fight or flight instinct, and prosperity.

This chakra is associated with the color red. It is located at the base of the spine and contains the energy there and surrounding the legs, feet, and gonads. It is connected to your sense of smell, the first sense you are aware of when you are born.

When your root chakra is balanced, you will feel secure, abundant, comfortable with yourself, centered, calm, grounded, and connected to nature and the earth.

When your root chakra is imbalanced, you may experience feelings of insecurity, anger, disconnection, depression, shortage of patience, nervousness, greed, unnecessary fear, and lack. When this imbalance manifests in our physical bodies, it may appear as frequent illness, obesity, eating disorders, constipation, knee troubles, sciatica, and even hemorrhoids.

Since the root chakra is where the dormant Kundalini energy lives and rises from when awakened, it is important to recognize the qualities of the chakra and its connection to all the other chakras. However, one must not put all emphasis on this energy and here is why: Kundalini awakening begins here, but it may also end in the root chakra. Some experiences show that it can be the last chakra to truly awaken. The rest of the transformation through the chakras may occur first but in order for true balance to be achieved, the energy of Kundalini must return to the beginning to where the source of the energy awakening began.

The Second Chakra — Svadhisthana

The second chakra is also often called the sacral chakra. Its Sanskrit name means "sweetness". It is the element of Water. It is the place of emotion and sexuality. It is the right "To Feel". This is the place of pleasure, fluid movement, creativity, and passion.

This chakra is associated with the color orange and is located in the area just below the navel in your lower abdomen and is associated with the bladder, female reproductive organs, lymphatic system, and pelvis. It is connected to the sense of taste.

When your sacral chakra is balanced, you will feel happy, joyful, creative, passionate, and capable of connecting physically. This is also where the drive to procreate exists.

When your sacral chakra is imbalanced, you may feel unworthiness, isolated, numb, stiff, overly sensitive and emotional.

You may also have a sexual addiction, or alternatively what is called sexual anorexia, hormone imbalance, and potential for miscarriages or difficulty conceiving.

This is a place where you block your emotions. Here is where you can really restrict the flow of energy as a whole. It is important to do the emotional work necessary, recovering lost feelings and sometimes re-experiencing them, so that you can heal and release them as you continue your awakening journey. Ultimately, when you heal and unblock your sacral chakra, you can allow a healthy flow of your emotional energy so you can really experience pleasure through body movement and sexuality.

Unblocking your sacral chakra can allow you to experience change, growth, and connection with your passionate self.

The Third Chakra — Manipura

The third chakra is also known as the solar plexus chakra. Its Sanskrit name means "lustrous gem." It is the element of Fire. It is power and it is energy. It is the right "To Act". This is the place of personal power, the strength of will, and sense of purpose.

This chakra is associated with the color yellow and it is located between the area just below the navel and the base of the sternum. The physical feature associated with the solar chakra is the adrenal glands. Your adrenal glands regulate metabolism, blood pressure, and your immune system.

When the chakra is in balance, you will feel energy and drive, confidence, sense of respect for others, as well as respect for the self, active and cheerful disposition, and a strong sense of purpose.

An imbalance of the solar plexus chakra can represent as an arrogant demeanor, demanding attitude, overbearing sensibilities, and addictions. The opposite side of imbalance would look like a deficiency of energy, a feeling of helplessness, a feeling of weakness, timidity, and submissive life approach.

This chakra demonstrates a significant turning point in Kundalini awakening as it will cause a profound shift in your intentions, intuitions, self-value and your ability to see beauty in the world. This is where judgment, biases, and prejudice melt away, first with the self and then the whole world around you. This is where you begin to feel your Kundalini power, but there is still so much more to go through.

The Fourth Chakra — Anahata

The fourth chakra is also known as the heart chakra. The Sanskrit name for this chakra translates to mean "unstruck", or unhurt, unbeaten. It is the element of Air. It is love and relationships. It is the right "To Love". This is the place of compassion for the self and others, acceptance of the self and others, and balance in all relationships.

This chakra is associated with the color green and is located in the center of the chest, behind the heart and in the spine. The physical component to this chakra is the thymus gland and lymph system which help regulate immunity and help fight disease and illness.

When the heart chakra is in balance, you will feel love, compassion, interconnectedness, acceptance, life will flow smoothly, and there will be a general feeling of affection for everyone and everything- Universal love.

If the heart chakra is imbalanced, it can express this through excessiveness or deficiency. A deficient heart chakra can often look like low self-worth or low self-esteem, melancholy, isolation, depression, inability to breathe deeply. Excessive heart chakra energy shows itself in the form of co-dependency, clingy behavior and too much caretaking of others.

Interestingly, like with the extremes listed above, the heart chakra can spontaneously open for energetic flow from a newly experienced, deep love of someone, and on the other end, extreme loss or grief can cause a shift and crack open.

Regardless of what causes the initial awakening of the heart chakra, be it the Kundalini awakening process, falling in love, or grieving a loss, it is sure to be an emotional roller-coaster. This can be aided with the Kundalini practices outlined in this book.

The Fifth Chakra — Vishuddhi

The fifth chakra is also called the throat chakra. The Sanskrit name for this chakra translated is "purification." It is the element of Ether or sound. It is communication. It is the right "To Speak". This is the place of self-expression, speaking, soul song and the ability to communicate with others.

The color associated with this chakra is blue and it is located at the throat. There are several physical features connected to this chakra such as the already mentioned throat, jaw, and neck, thyroid gland, teeth, ears, and esophagus; everything associated with speaking and listening.

When this chakra is balanced, you can enjoy clear and truthful self-expression, honest and good communication, creative expression and affinity with self and others. There is also an ability to comprehend the balance of opposite forces with reverence, accepting the value of both light and dark, high and low and they each have a vital role in the harmony of all life energy.

When this chakra experiences imbalances or blockages, it can manifest as difficulty expressing oneself, inability to release wounds, pain or trauma because of suppressed emotions, sore throat, difficulty hearing, actual ear problems, tight neck and shoulders, and stagnant creative flow.

This chakra has a great deal to do with sound so a lot of the methods for clearing blockages, or opening and activating the throat chakra utilize singing or chanting, rhythm entrainment, and sound vibration.

The Sixth Chakra — Ajna

The sixth chakra is often called the brow chakra or third eye. The Sanskrit name for this chakra translates to mean "perceive", or to know. It is the element of Light. It is visual perception, intuition, clairvoyance. It is the right "To See". This is the place of imagination, thought, telepathy, vision, rational logic.

The sixth chakra is associated with the color indigo and is situated between the eyes or behind the eyebrows. Its physical attribute is the pituitary and pineal gland. The pituitary gland regulates hormone secretions, while the pineal gland is involved in regulation of sleep patterns and circadian rhythms.

When the sixth chakra is balanced, there are great abilities in perception, your mind is at ease and can process thought quickly, improved memory and intelligence, lacking fear of death, you have a strong connection to your intuition and can have clairvoyant and telepathic abilities surface.

An imbalance in the sixth chakra can manifest as headaches, mental health issues and illness such as hallucinations and nightmares, paranoia, anxiety, and delusions. Because of its connection to sight and the eyes, it can also present itself as poor sight or visual perception.

Once this chakra becomes open and blockages begin to clear, energy can travel back down through the lower chakras for continued healing and cleansing, as there will likely be unresolved energy blocks still needing cleansing. That is why the Kundalini awakening process is an ongoing journey with the self.

The Seventh Chakra — Sahasrara

The seventh chakra is also often called the crown chakra. The Sanskrit name for this chakra translates to mean "thousand-fold". It is the element of thought. It is expanded consciousness. It is the right "To Know". This is the place of understanding, of enlightenment.

The crown chakra is associated with the color violet and is located at the top of the head at the cerebral cortex. The physical component of this chakra included the brain, hands, nervous system and in part the pituitary gland, creating a link to the sixth chakra.

When the seventh chakra is balanced, you will have an expanded consciousness that will lead to a transcendence of barriers projected by humanity and the laws of nature, have a greater understanding and acceptance of death, mortality and the immortality of the soul, increased and heightened spiritual gifts and capabilities, and the creation of miracles.

If your crown chakra is blocked, it can manifest as migraines, headaches, and general tension around the head. You may also feel alienated or isolated, suffer boredom, have an apathetic quality, disconnection and a lack of comprehension or ability to learn and retain new information. It can also go in the direction of being a bit spacey, "in your head" all the time, and sometimes overly intellectual which can prevent your ability to attain pure-consciousness.

The balancing or opening of this chakra in Kundalini awakening is closely connected to the third eye. The ability to transcend and experience enlightenment is the moving away from smaller patterns to welcome a deeper, broader perspective, one that encompasses all life and all matter, beyond the confines of limited thoughts and beliefs that keep our kundalini locked and dormant.

From the Root to the Head and Beyond

The system as a whole is a beautiful, throbbing and constantly vibrating energetic life force of its own. This chakra energy is always present and always fluctuating. When the Kundalini energy is activated at the base of your spine in your first chakra, you begin the upward journey that will cause you to face all the elements, qualities, blocks, deficiencies and excesses of your chakras. It is the beginning of healing and awakening to your own divine light and energy to become one with the power of creation. What you discover on this path, the path through the chakras, will be how you come into contact with the true nature of yourself and all things.

Knowing about each chakra is important for the awakening process as it will give you the understanding to listen to your body. It is also important because they are the essential, energetic part of your being directly linked to Kundalini awakening experience. Take some time to really listen to each part of your body, each chakra system and develop a relationship to each energy so that you can be connected to the whole of your subtle body.

Chapter 12: Enhancing Psychic Abilities

Psychic Abilities and How to Awaken Them

Clairvoyant forces can be grown normally. Everybody has an intuition, and keeping in mind that some have it more emphatically than others, we as a whole can wakeful that sense through training. Contemplation obviously is an extraordinary spot to begin. It's been said on numerous occasions that contemplation is useful for the psyche, body, soul, and in general prosperity. Putting in a couple of calm minutes independent from anyone else every day truly can help. Work on breathing methods too. Breath gradually done in an example that feels great to you. Add incense and candles to the experience too.

Keeping a diary is another smart thought for those keen on expanding their clairvoyant capacities. Record all that you experience during reflection. Record the majority of your emotions. Each picture or felt that goes through your brain may in the end synchronize with the world, so give nearer consideration to what your psyche is letting you know. The capacity to plainly picture occasions, individuals, and places in your inner being is an unquestionable requirement on the off chance that you need increasingly clairvoyant forces. Return and rehash your words frequently. In time, you should begin seeing the things you compose relating with genuine occasions.

A significant number of the stages are related with the intertwining of the enthusiastic, vitality body and the profound body, which is an imperative hidden piece of the advancement procedure.

1.Life Crisis

This stage doesn't really need to happen to everybody on the clairvoyant way in the event that they pay heed to the stones at a beginning time. Be that as it may, the move towards wishing to create on a clairvoyant level is frequently gone before by a real existence dramatization. This can be anything from a confounded adolescence to an ongoing separation.

2. Increased Awareness

This is the point at which you begin to see things out of the edge of your eye. This can likewise begin with seeing 'masses' of shading or whirling energies. For other people, it will be the start of hearing messages in your psyche, clear dreams, hunches, and thinking you are either going frantic or the brain is playing stunts. Frequently individuals disregard the stones here, and reject what their increased faculties are attempting to let them know.

3. Touchiness

Winding up progressively touchy to analysis and other individuals' perspectives. At this stage you start to realize that you can feel other individuals' sentiments. Perplexity and a feeling of, 'am I ordinary' win at this stage.

4. Looking

The quest for material that clarifies the peculiar encounters starts. This is frequently done discreetly through dread of derision. Likewise a powerful urge to discover 'similarly invested' people starts. It is at this stage you start to truly scrutinize your rational soundness! This is the final turning point. From this phase forward you will go through your time on earth looking for answers to life's inquiries. There might be rests in the middle of yet you will consistently be interested. It ends up like a tingle you can't scratch.

5. Beginning to support yourself

Be careful! The accommodating will abruptly fire going to bat for themselves and won't take any garbage. This might be present moment as it is just the beginning. A solid establishment has not yet been developed yet the wheels will have been gotten under way.

6. Feeling alone/misjudged

At this stage the creating clairvoyant has normally discovered material to halfway clarify their advantage and individuals of a similarly invested nature. Tragically at this stage, those frequently nearest to the individual will need to demolish their accomplice's/companion's new intrigue since they feel (however won't let it out) compromised by the new 'side interest'. The mystic will regularly be approached by a 'concerned' relative about how they are getting into a mysterious or being mentally conditioned, and how it is all gobbledegook. In the event that you don't have this stage you are extremely fortunate!!

This prompts a very befuddled mystic. Is it wrong to proceed? What would it be advisable for me to do? Am I distraught? Generally the choice is to continue discreetly and not impart the recently discovered learning to your quick friends.

7. I can't do it

Sentiments of uncertainty surface very well at this stage. The creating clairvoyant sees others moving at a quicker speed. They can't work out how to speed their own advancement however become progressively crippled due to the speed their mystic companions are moving at around them.

For some the inverse may occur, this will be they believe they are moving too immediately, alarmed by the experience and needing to back it off or shut it off in light of the fact that the duty feels overpowering.

Envision awakening into an abnormal and obscure world to you. On the off chance that you are one of the fortunate rare sorts of people who might be very inquisitive and would appreciate awakening in the new, the new would seem an overwhelming spot until you had became acclimated to it. For some, they start to wake up in this new world, they attempt to deny themselves the reality they are awakening some place distinctive in the expectation things can remain the equivalent, the recognizable and surely understood, 'safe place'. This will proceed until the creating clairvoyant is never again terrified and wishes to grasp the 'new world' they are awakening to – this can take a few while.

We have all sooner or later in our life dreaded change. The stunt in defeating the dread of progress is to pause for a minute to quick advance life to how it will be on the off chance that we continue as before. Life can't change except if we change, only trusting it will change prompts dissatisfaction. In your brain, quick forward your life to how it will be once change has occurred. You will before long observe change is an energizing alternative!

8. Needing quiet/to be distant from everyone else

The faculties are as yet honing, as they are doing so it is likely at this stage the creating clairvoyant turns out to be exceptionally delicate to boisterous commotions, they may discover they can't stand the radio playing or the sound of raised voices. Regularly they will need to be in open space or feel a solid should be in the farmland. An expanded wish to spend periods alone considering or 'gazing out the kitchen window.' Your body is revealing to you it wishes to ponder. During this stage it is important to locate an ordinary calm spot during the day to maintain a strategic distance from touchiness.

9. Acknowledgment that your activity/conditions are not directly for you

This is the start of figuring out how to see the blocks!! Frequently individuals will hold up until they are made excess or sacked (the stone) before they can see they have outgrown their activity/conditions/relationship or that their work environment or home doesn't coordinate with their freshly discovered mindfulness. This is regularly a shocking stage since it is tied in with understanding that your life has frequently been a trade off (not generally) up until this point. The troublesome piece is the mental fortitude to give up and proceed onward.

Traveling through this stage regularly turns into a hindrance for a great many people and postpones their advancement. This stage is tied in with splitting ceaselessly from the choices 'made for you' throughout everyday life and 'what you have done to satisfy another'. It is tied in with breaking free of the vocation you picked in light of the fact that it satisfied your folks, the relationship you remained in for accommodation or the activity you do, for the cash.

Likely the most significant factor in picking the mystic way and building up your expertise as well as could be expected; is about genuineness. You can't be a genuinely bona fide mystic except if you are straightforward with yourself. The individuals who are not fair with themselves regularly dread the clairvoyant way. The individuals who are straightforward with themselves grasp it!

10. Feeling deserted

This part doesn't really happen to everybody on the mystic way.

At this stage loved ones begin to leave your life or they seem, by all accounts, to be leaving. The creating mystic never again feels associated with those they have been partner with for quite a long time. A mind-blowing structures start to break down. All that you thought to be genuine/are connected to, self-destruct.

How discouraging!! This is really a fabulous stage, giving you ensure you stretch your view past the present circumstance. How would you fix a neglected structure? Well you don't! First you need to wreck it with the goal that you manufacture another, more grounded one in its place.

This stage is tied in with seeing through any hallucinations. Through this stage we find what is genuine. We genuinely reveal to ourselves lies! We let ourselves know all is well when it's most certainly not. We disclose to ourselves it's terrible when obviously it's alright. At the point when all is detracted from us we start to comprehend the excellence of the Universe. We build up an extraordinary comprehension of what is extremely significant and figure out how to profoundly welcome the little things throughout everyday life. Incidental data progresses toward becoming random data once this stage is finished. What appeared to be wrecking doesn't convey a similar feeling it did beforehand.

Wild weeping for no obvious explanation is a piece of this stage. This is on the grounds that the cells of the body are beginning to lose old memory, clearing a path for the solid capacity to see into your very own and other individuals' lives.

11. Expanded capacity

The clairvoyant faculties more often than not at this point are creating with a generally excellent and firm establishment. The capacity to 'read' individuals is regularly actually very solid by this stage.

12. De-tox

This phase for certain individuals comes from the get-go, for other people, it comes significantly later. In the event that you are overlooking it a physical ailment will frequently need to surface to demonstrate to you (a stone). The period of time you have been disregarding the need for this the heavier the physical sickness.

At this stage the time has come to tidy up your body and on the off chance that it has not occurred as of now, your musings. As the capacity to channel higher energies than your own, builds, it is fundamental the channel the energies are utilizing, is a 'spotless' one. In the event that it isn't, as happens with a ton of mystic's not decent physical disease starts to happen. On the off chance that you decline to de-tox, the impact is somewhat similar to stuffing a potato up a fumes pipe.

To de-tox means fasting for a couple of days. There are a wide range of fasts you can do, from just drinking water for a day or somewhere in the vicinity, to having dark colored rice for breakfast, lunch and supper for as long as ten days. Do a colon rinse, eat a lot of crisp products of the soil. Eat less sugar and meat. Limit your caffeine admission. Avoid low vitality nourishment, for example, takeaways and microwave suppers. In the event that you smoke, drink a lot of liquor or are dependant on any type of medications (lawful or illicit) at that point either stop or get help to stop.

Kindly note, ingesting unlawful medications is a low vitality practice; in this manner adverse to yourself as well as any individual you might peruse for. Because of the reality it is a low vitality act, you will draw in low vitality soul, and you won't have the option to continue your vitality at a sufficiently high vibration to channel effectively. It would be an over the top bounce from being low vitality to directing high vitality. Long haul, individuals who do this will cut off the lights will blow!

13. Needing to support everybody

This stage may seem as if it is an extraordinary spot to be. In established truth it isn't. You can't support anybody, just yourself, you can offer individuals an 'advantage' not a 'hold up'. On the off chance that you attempt and drag an individual along to a spot inside where they truly would prefer not to be nevertheless you think it is best for them, stop it – disregard them!! Concentrate on 'oneself', your 'self'. Individuals are fine as they may be, you just reserve the option to change yourself – disregard them!

Those in your life be that as it may, may oblige it for some time to be well mannered. Because you have begun to locate this newly discovered information you figure the world should know, you will in case you're not cautious, get the 'crackpot' status inside your family or friend network. You reserve no privilege to smash things down the throat of others. On the off chance that they are intrigued they will inquire. In the event that you do slam information down individuals' necks (there will be the allurement) be readied on the grounds that at some stage you will get your speculations shot somewhere around the 'life is just what you can see' doubter. In the event that/when you get to this stage, contending may be a misuse of your vitality. Acknowledge and watch their perspectives as they may be, they're qualified for them. You wouldn't care for your assessment shot down so it's out of line to take shots at or back at theirs.

For the most part at this stage the creating mystic concerning this subject won't be tremendously certain inside oneself. You will know when you are, on the grounds that you won't have a need to advise others how to be, and they will start to have a profound regard for your enthusiasm for clairvoyant improvement. It's practically unexpected in that regard.

This stage is a trial of how consistent with yourself you are. Hardly any individuals like to be 'lectured' on how they should carry on with their life, so recollect LEAVE THEM ALONE, regardless of the amount you can see they are going along an inappropriate way. Offer exhortation ONLY on the off chance that they inquire! Stay away from the, 'let you know so' when they've committed their error. In the end they will approach you first for your mystic exhortation before they act (keep it unprejudiced) when they have seen a couple of times, your expectations have been exact. Meanwhile, center around proceeding to create yourself.

14. Know all

At this stage you 'know everything'. The creating mystic ends up exhausted with the techniques they are learning. Feel their gathering is keeping them down; they don't have anything more to learn. The conviction begins to set in that they have encountered enough to proceed onward and go only it, away from their companions.

A few people lose companions in this stage and become seen as aloof, regardless of whether on knowing the past they are believed to be all knowing. As this stage turns out to be progressively built up, the clairvoyant gets to the phase of 'the more you realize the less you have to state', inevitably increasing extraordinary regard for their capacities as the need to lecture vanishes – an incredible spot to be.

15. Clearing

This is the stage the fun truly begins!! The clearing stage is the point at which every one of the things you have never managed, or every one of the things you discover startling, start to raise their head. Your extremely most exceedingly terrible feelings of trepidation become substances and every one of your weaknesses pound at you. The more you have overlooked them throughout everyday life, the more articulated the manner in which the Universe will indicate them to you for clearing. The path forward with this stage is to grasp and respect the clearing stage, for this is the thing that will truly transform yourself for the better until the end of time!

This stage as a rule includes a great deal of crying and outrageous' of feeling. During this stage it is regularly best to remain with your present occupation and conditions. The very underlying foundations of what you thought was steady will be shaken. It is regularly at this stage the creating mystic thinks they have to change the facades (Job, relationship and so forth) to satisfy them. This isn't the situation, accusing these circumstances, as the wellspring of your despondency will slow the procedure. Stick with 'preparing' the emotions you are experiencing, at exactly that point change the facades if your sentiments are as yet the equivalent.

Contingent upon the creating mystic, this procedure can last a few while and will occur pair with a portion of different stages. During this procedure, the creating clairvoyant will acknowledge it's anything but a maverick's procedure and come back to their companions inside their advancement bunch for assistance and counsel.

16. Leap forward

After the clearing procedure (which can take some time) the mystic turns out to be especially insightful. They can 'see' what is happening inside/for somebody at a hundred paces. This is on the grounds that anything that was impeding opening up to a genuine condition of being, has been expelled during the clearing procedure. There is then nothing halting you!!

Chapter 13: How To Heal Your Chakras

The variations of these techniques are dependent upon you, your preferences, and where you are going to seek additional help. There are some tools that are best handled by people who are trained in their skill, but you can actually learn many of these skills and take all of your healing into your own hands.

Starting off with your first ideas for healing, you can begin to shift a lot of your energy by going to see some different specialists who can begin to help you unblock your energies on a deep level.

How to Heal Your Chakras on Your Own

All of the above methods work well in addition to what you can do on your own time at home. The practice of healing the self requires consistency and devotion. I trust you are already capable of knowing that it is in your hands and that you get to decide how much and how often, but if you are really hoping to inspire change, everyday practice on some level is ideal.

Mantras

Mantras are an amazingly powerful tool. They are simple sounds, words, or phrases that elicit a specific internal and external consequence. There are a lot of mantras out there and it can be confusing to decide what mantras work best for which situations.

The point of mantras is to inform the mind of what you want. Thoughts can be very hurtful, accusatory, and demeaning to who you are and what you want. The idea of the mantra is to rephrase the thoughts that are keeping you down or low so that your mind forms newer, more emotionally intelligent neural pathways to think on.

A mantra doesn't have to be a specific word or phrase to have meaning.

Have you ever heard of the classic word, 'Om'? Om is used quite regularly in yoga practices and other meditative experiences and it helps you to connect to deeper energy within your body, and it is also a mantra.

Mantras are energy and as you will discover later, they are an excellent way to transform your energy from negative to positive and to keep your chakras in a good balance.

Meditations

Meditation is no new thing. It is one of the hottest buzz words, still. The work you do around meditation is a lot simpler than many people might think. The basics are that you sit in stillness, clear your mind, and enter a present state with yourself. This is not as easy as it sounds because we have a lot of thoughts, feelings, worries, and so forth that make it hard to stay centered and focus only on the emptiness in the mind.

When you take the time to meditate, you are taking the time to connect to your energy and then make it possible to hear it, understand what is going on in your life, and clear anything that is causing you problems or difficulties.

Crystals

Crystals are strong, energetic objects. They are made by the Earth and they carry positive healing vibrations and higher frequencies. There are so many different varieties and colors and each has a different purpose and meaning. You can find hundreds and hundreds of them and learn as much as you want about the power of each gemstone or crystal.

You can actually place them over any one of your chakras and let it sit there for 10-30 minutes while you close your eyes and meditate. The energy of the crystal connects with the energy of the chakra and from there will help to purge, balance and transmute the energy of that placement.

There are even specific stones for a specific chakra. The crystals will usually share the qualities of the chakra so that when you are applying that crystal to the chakra it connects to, you are informing that chakra of how it wants to feel through the energy of the stone.

Exploring crystals will help you find what you need to expedite the transformation process. Crystals are like putting a magnifying glass on the issue and burning it out with light, as is the case with Reiki on the chakras.

Reiki and Yoga

As you have already learned, Reiki is a healing method that has evolved from ancient wisdom and techniques. It is often applied through service with someone known as a practitioner or a Master who has a higher degree of Reiki training. One thing you can actually do to help your healing journey is to get trained to do Reiki on yourself.

The techniques are divided into three levels of learning and the first level is for students who are only interested in practicing this healing technique on their own bodies. It can be a very helpful and powerful method for healing quickly and you can find a Reiki Master to give you the lessons in your local community. You may have to pay for the class and it will likely take the length of a weekend workshop, but after that, you will have another excellent tool to heal yourself with.

Yoga is also something you can teach yourself and inventing your own daily routine or yoga ritual will provide you with ongoing healing of the chakra energy and keeping it a good balance. There are even yoga poses that are specific to each chakra so if you feel like you are out of balance in one area or chakra, you can design a yoga practice that will be specific to the needs of that chakra.

Either, or both, of these practices, would be an excellent addition to working with meditations, mantras, and crystals. The more you do, the faster you heal.

Additional Tips, Hints, and Ideas

- Spend time in nature, hiking, walking, lying in the grass, gardening, or anything else that you like to do outdoors.
- Dance, dance, dance, like nobody, is watching.
- Play a musical instrument, even if you think you are terrible and have no skill. The point is to make sound, not to be a pop star.
- Eat well. This means fresh vegetables, fruits, nuts, and lean meats with lots of water and low intake of alcohol, sugar, caffeine, and processed foods with ingredients you can't

pronounce the names of easily.

- Hobbies. Find your hobbies and passions and make them a part of your life.
- Listen to music, any kind of music.
- Take time to go to places you have never been to before, even if it is in your hometown or city.
- Look at art, in museums, in books, or online.
- Get involved in some kind of community service.
- Take a class you have always wanted to take. Expand your knowledge.
- Design your daily life to include only what you want to do, not just what you feel like you have to, even when it means working a lot.
- Share your stories and experiences with other people.
- Try something you have always been afraid of.
- Practice with your intuition and see how well you already know what you think you don't.
- Sleep and rest well.

All of these tips and pointers seem like common sense, but all too often each of us forgets what we can do to improve our energy and our health. These activities are actually helpful ways to alter your chakra energy for the better. When you give your energy what it actually wants and needs, you are offering yourself healing and balance.

Chapter 14: Astral Travel and Clairvoyance

Astral travel is defined by some as the ability to voluntarily have an out of body experience. This concept theorizes that they soul is capable of traveling around outside of one's physical body, that the soul cannot be trapped within one's physical form and may be projected at will. Most people experience astral travel during near- death experiences or during times of great illness. With the enhancement of psychic abilities, it is entirely possible to perform astral travel at will. Astral projection usually only lasts for a few hours, though it may feel much longer (more like days or months) to the one who is experiencing astral projection.

Astral Travel is often described as "dreaming while awake", and many consider this concept to be like having an out of body experience. Astral travel is your mind's ability to experience your surroundings without being limited to your physical body. Astral travel allows your soul to be free from your physical body in order to travel the universe freely. While experiencing astral travel, you control the astral projection's length of time. During astral projection, you remain in control of your mind and are therefore able to steer yourself away from any source of negativity that you may encounter. The ability to see and communicated with those who have passed away is not an uncommon experience during astral projection, and those who are able to achieve astral travel are also able to visit various countries, planets, and even other realms during their projections.

An individual's soul or astral body is said to be connected to the individual's physical body by an astral cord (also known as the silver cord) that can stretch to an almost infinite length. The silver cord cannot be severed, with the only exception being in the occurrences of death.

1) Sitting in a quiet environment and in a relaxed position, perform meditation in order to relieve all tension and stress from your body.

2) Lie on your back on a completely flat surface, and close your eyes lightly.

3) Remain relaxed until you hear or feel the vibrations often experienced during meditative exercises. Keeping your eyes closed, imagine your astral

body rising out above the limits of your physical body.

Clairvoyance (Psychic Vision)

One of the most popular forms of psychic ability is clairvoyance, and (especially in books or television) it is often referred to as "the gift". The ability of clairvoyance originates within the sixth chakra (the Third Eye) in the areas of the brain biologically recognized as the pituitary and pineal glands. While everyone has the ability to possess some psychic ability, not everyone will have the same ability to be a clairvoyant individual. The majority of individuals are born with relatively strong clairvoyant abilities, but most people lose these abilities by a certain (often young) age. This can be demonstrated when children claim to see deceased relatives (even those whom they have never met), when they have seemingly realistic "imaginary" friends, or when children seem to intuitively know when something is wrong with the adults surrounding them.

Clairvoyance is defined, simply, as the ability or skill of psychic vision. A more in-depth definition of this skill can be described as "perceiving things or events in the future or beyond normal sensory contact". Clairvoyancc is sometimes referred to as "second sight" or "psychic sight" and translates to meaning "clear seeing". This skill is described by those who experience it as the reception of intuitive clues, often in the form of symbols, images, or visions. Some clairvoyants claim that certain tools are able to help them in order to easily connect with or strengthen their abilities: the more common tools for this purpose are tea leaves, tarot cards, runes, or even crystals. Precognition is a form clairvoyance in which an individual is able to foresee events before they happen. Precognitive abilities usually present themselves as visions while one is asleep.

Chapter 15: Activate And Decalcify Your Pineal Gland

The pineal gland or your third eye holds remarkable power. However, only a few people can tap into this power and use it effectively. Many people simply have an underdeveloped third eye. But, the good news is that there are exercises that you can do to strengthen your third eye so you can start using and enjoying its immense power. Let us discuss them one by one:

- *Who is it?*

This is something that you can do every time your phone rings or beeps. Simply ask yourself, "Who is it?" Pay attention to what you see in your mind's eye. Do you see any image or impressions? Be open to receiving messages. This is how you can connect to your intuition. You should also realize that you have a strong intuition and that you only have to learn to connect to it. Of course, this technique is not limited to calls or texts on your phone. You can also adjust it a bit and use it in other ways. For example, if you hear a knock or any sound at night, you can ask, "What is it?" and pay attention to any messages that you get from your intuition. The important thing is to start connecting to your intuition once again.

- Forehead press

This technique is becoming popular these days. This, however, does not work on everyone but it is still worth trying. This will allow you some specks of prana in the air. They usually appear as little dots or any form of white light. The steps are as follows:

Place your index finger in the area between the eyebrows where the Ajna chakra is. Press it gently and maintain pressure for about 50 seconds. Slowly remove your finger, blink your eyes around five times, and look at a blank wall. Just focus lightly and try to see with your peripheral vision. Do you see little dots or any specks of white light? This is prana in the air.

To help you see the energy, you might want to do this in a dimly lit room. Look at a wall with a neutral background. This is a good way to use your third eye to see energy, but it is not a recommended method to strengthen the Ajna chakra. Still, this is something that is worth trying, especially if you just want to see prana.

- Visual screen

This is a good technique to use for visualization exercises. To locate the visual screen, close your eyes and look slightly upward. With eyes closed, look at the area of the Ajna chakra. This is your visual screen. You can project anything that you like to this screen, especially images. You can consider this as some form of internal magic mirror.

The main purpose of this visual screen is for your visualization exercises. Here is a simple exercise you can do to increase your concentration and willpower:

Assume a meditative posture and relax. Now, look at your visual screen. Imagine an apple floating in front of you. Now, just focus on this apple and do not entertain any other thoughts. This is just like the breathing meditation. However, instead of focusing on your breath, focus on the apple in your visual screen.
When you are ready to end this meditation, simply visualized the apple slowly fade away and gently open your eyes.

You are also welcome to use any other object for this meditation. If you do not want to use an apple, you can visualize an orange or even an elephant. The important thing is to have a point of visual focus for this meditation.

- Charging with the fire element

Remember that the intuition is associated with the pineal gland, in the pineal gland is the third eye chakra. Now, this third eye chakra is associated with the fire element. Therefore, you can empower your third eye chakra by charging it with the element of fire. This is a powerful technique so be sure to use it carefully. The steps are as follows:

Assume a meditative posture and relax. Close your eyes. Now, visualize the brilliant and powerful sun above you. This powerful sun is full of the element of fire. As you inhale, see and feel that you are drawing the energy from the sun. Let the energy charge your third eye chakra and empower it. Do this with every inhalation. The more that you charge your third eye, the more that it lights up and become more powerful. Have faith that with every inhalation, you become more and more intuitive.

Keep in mind that this is a powerful technique. If you are just starting out, it is suggested that you only do up to 10 inhalations in the beginning. You can then add one or two more inhalations every week. You will know if you can execute this technique properly because you will feel pressure on your forehead in the area of your third eye chakra. Take note that you should not just visualize your third eye chakra getting stronger, but you should also be conscious that your intuition becomes more powerful the more that you charge your third eye. The power of visualization should be accompanied by your intention.

- Note

It should be noted that the Ajna chakra and crown chakra are closely connected. If you want to improve your intuition, it is only right that you also work on your crown chakra. Of course, this does not mean that you should ignore your other chakras. Again, the whole chakra system is important to your spiritual development and to the awakening of the kundalini.

Conclusion

Thank you for making it through to the end of Kundalini Awakening, let's hope it was informative and able to provide you with all of the tools you need to achieve your goals whatever they may be.

The next step is to continue your practice and see where your path leads. The exercises in this book are rooted in an ancient and mysterious past of Indian culture. They literally could be practiced for years without finding an end. Even the simplest meditation exercise can be practiced for decades without losing its potency and power. This shows the immense amount of potential that humans have to transform their lives and empower themselves that these practices have to offer.

The next step is to reaffirm every day that you are on your way to becoming a better, fuller you. Believe in yourself and your ability to make the changes necessary to realize your goals. Once you've removed the clutter from your mind, you will turn overthinking into focused achieving, each and every day. You may have heard many times over, "easier said than done." Well, you should be excited to learn how to do what you set your mind to do. You've wanted to make a change for a long time. Taking the steps to make your goals come to fruition is something many people never achieve.

It is times like this, after having taken a big step forward in my life, when I begin to reflect on how far I've come. It is hard to appreciate your progress sometimes when you are in the heat of battle and struggling every day during the beginning, middle, or even near the end of your efforts. There is nothing better than stepping up onto that final rung and looking down to see all of those completed steps in your wake.

Remember when you were sitting at square one, unable to free yourself from the chains of overthinking? I know it well—I've been there myself. It takes a great deal of courage to stand up and say, I'm ready to make a change. It saddens me to think that many people continue to overthink and overanalyze throughout their entire lives, missing out on the experiences and appreciation that a free mind can realize. It is easy to slip into the comfortable habits of mindless eating, checking a phone or tablet every few minutes, and going to bed later and later until your system is all out of sorts. Sometimes, it seems too easy to give in and let what's easy overshadow what's worth working for. You don't have to be a slave to overthinking, and maybe it's possible for you to take what you've learned and help change lives around you.

Perhaps you know someone who seems to be struggling with overthinking, stressing out about everyday challenges and stress just like you were at the beginning of your journey. Consider reaching out and sharing what you've learned. Nothing feels better than sharing new knowledge with someone who can use it to make the positive changes you've seen happen in yourself. Maybe it's a coworker, a spouse, or a close friend. Many people from different walks of life will benefit from the changes laid out in this book, so why not share your story!

PART TWO

Kundalini Awakening

GUIDED MEDITATION TO DEVELOP EMOTIONAL INTELLIGENCE, PSYCHIC ABILITIES, AWARENESS, INTUITION, AWAKEN THIRD EYE CHAKRA & CHAKRA FOR BEGINNERS. ACTIVATE BREATHING & HEALING BODY.

Introduction

All human beings possess and innate intellectual mechanism in their genetic makeup that makes it possible for them to tap into their hidden divine power, illumination and genius. This mechanism, or energy, is called Kundalini.

The word Kundalini originates from Sanskrit and means the coiled one. In fact, in ancient Eastern religions the energy is depicted as coiled around the vertebrae column base three times and a half like a serpent. In these etchings, the coiled serpent rouses from slumber from the vertebrae column while one is meditating deeply or praying.

In its simplest terms Kundalini is the basic energy, also known as Shakti, positioned at the spinal cord base. It is an energy that manipulates and runs the spiritual and intellectual life force (prana) of all human beings. When awakened, it promotes spiritual awakening and attaining of intellectual maturity. Though the energy is naturally present in everyone, it is not that easy to deliberately awaken it because as humans we have intellectual and spiritual blockages that hinder awakening of our kundalini

Awakening can be likened to an out-of-body experience that can be likened to having an electric current running up and down the spinal cord. Once achieved, Kundalini awakening leads to spiritual awakening, freedom of the soul and awakening of creativity and freedom.

Little is understood about this energy because it is an unconscious energy. One can go through their life without ever knowing they possess Kundalini or even experiencing its immense benefits. Kundalini is a dormant energy that is not necessary for day to day living, but once awakened it enhances life beyond compare.

Chapter 1: Understanding the Kundalini

Kundalini is a potent, fiery energy that is located at the bottom of the spine of each person. This energy is both powerful and intelligent, and it energizes the body while heightening our consciousness. Its name derives from the Sanskrit Kundala, a word that means coiled. When dormant, the Kundalini remains coiled around the tailbone until it climbs up to the head. This awakening can happen spontaneously or voluntarily.

Awakening the Kundalini results in spiritual enlightenment, which bestows upon the person many gifts, some of which are increased strength, improved health, tranquility, bliss, wisdom, and even supernatural abilities. Many belief systems have equated Kundalini activation with spiritual liberation and the complete fulfillment of man's potential; thus, a lot of people are practicing techniques to rouse their own Kundalini.

The idea of the Kundalini or Shakti originates from Hinduism, but some say that it has its counterpart in other religions – for example, Christianity calls it the Holy Spirit or Pentecostal Fire, Judaism refers to it as Shekinah, in Islam it is Sakina, in Egypt its name is Sekhem, and in Gnostic traditions it is the Goddess or Divine Mother. Taoists describe it as the greater/greatest Kan (Water) and Li (fire), the Kalahari gave it the name Num, and the Kaballists refer to it as the "secret fire".

The energy is said to be a female energy that is naturally attracted to the masculine force in the top of the head or fontanel. The meeting of the two forces of the Divine Mother/Goddess and Divine Father/God is considered by some as a sacred marriage that bears the Son of God. Furthermore, some say that Jesus has successfully ignited this spiritual fire, thus he became the Christ or anointed one. This is also the reason why he was supposedly able to perform miracles and attain a divine status.

Although some people have attached religious ideas to Kundalini, there are also those who say that it is beyond any specific religion or culture. In fact, individuals from all kinds of backgrounds experience

Basically, Kundalini awakening deals with subtle energies (called as prana, chi, orgone, etheric energy, bio energy or vital energy) and the subtle human anatomy (ex: nadis, energy meridians, chakras, auras, energy fields, etc.).

According to Hindu and many other mystical systems of belief, everything has components that are non-physical and are inaccessible to the normal physical senses. Instead, they are usually perceived via extra-sensory perception. It is said that at certain conditions, they can cause effects that are perceivable by senses or gadgets – like light, heat, vibration, radiation, or fluctuations in random number generator results. Kundalini itself is a subtle energy that resides in the subtle energy body, with the coccyx or tailbone as its physical container.

The different kinds of subtle energies have their own characteristics and purposes. Kundalini in particular is thought of as a force that spurs rapid evolution. It is explained to be the driving force of a single fertilized egg transforming into billions of cells that are coordinated together to form the body of a live human.

After the baby has emerged from the womb, the Kundalini is still operational but in a subdued form. It may act in full force once more when the individual is genetically predisposed for it or if he/she has undergone certain experiences or spiritual practices.

When the Kundalini uncoils and awakens, it rises up the spine in the form of pulses, waves, sparks, or flames. It then taps to the energies of the Universe, which enter the body to cleanse and infuse the person with power. Although this may happen spontaneously, majority of people need to undergo certain processes to make this possible.

Although it is not yet fully understood why spontaneous awakenings occur, some guess that the subconscious mind, the soul, or the Divine knows that it is the right time to activate the dormant energy. Whatever the reason may be, it will cause changes in the person's life that will ultimately lead to the greater good.

Again, the essential purpose of the Kundalini is to help with evolution. It brings energy and directs the processes that are necessary to upgrade the individual so that he/she can cope with living at a higher level. Even when it is dormant, it still performs several functions, such as spark growth, generate sex drive and build consciousness. It energizes prana or vital energy so that it can carry sensations and impulses more effectively. However, the

Kundalini only works at its fullest when it reaches the crown of the head. Because of this, a person must have a clear Kundalini path; if not, he or she has to prepare the path for the energy. Otherwise, he or she will feel pain or pressure as the energy encounters blocks, or the Kundalini may not move at all.

Energy Blockages

Kundalini awakening becomes problematic when the energy encounters blocks along its path. Blocks may form as a result of:

- negativity
- repressed emotions
- psychological wounds
- rigid beliefs and attitudes
- afflictions
- attachments
- unprepared body

These blocks limit consciousness and energy, making it harder for Kundalini to perform in its full power. Thus, Kundalini awakening practices involves clearing blocks. Spontaneous awakening happens when these issues are resolved.

According to Yogic belief, there are two energetic channels (Nadis) along the spinal column called the Ida and the Pingala, and a hollow canal (Nadi) named as the Sushumna. The Kundalini lies dormant at the bottom of this column and coiled around the tailbone three and a half times. When it stirs awake, it pushes through the channel and peels off the layers that separate the mind from the ultimate reality.

Although the biological basis of the Kundalini is not yet understood, it is sometimes associated with the nervous system that comprises of the brain, the spinal cord, and the multitude of nerves in the body. These physical parts help produce sensation and awareness via the help of electrical signals. Because of its functions and behavior, the Kundalini may be related to the workings of the nervous system, and when the energy rises, it may pass through the spinal cord until it reaches into the brain. Once it's there, it may amplify the entire energy system of the person, bestowing new abilities and empowering existing ones.

Before that happens though, it must traverse through the channels whether they are physical or energetic. Since the Kundalini is a powerful force, it can cause damages when it gets stuck where it isn't supposed to be. This is one important reason why Kundalini awakening is notoriously risky.

Because of the potential dangers of Kundalini activation, many teachers warn students to not activate it without good reason, and simply being curious about it may cause regrets later on. It is best if you seek this only if you are ready to experience discomfort for the sake of refining your soul. It will also help to know more about it as much as you can, especially if you notice Kundalini activation symptoms in you already.

Symptoms of Blockages

The manifestation of blockages depends on where the Kundalini got stuck. It may feel as tightness, heat, tingling, or any kind of discomfort or unusual sensation in an area of the body. Sometimes, it may affect the aspect of life that corresponds to a troublesome chakra – an excessive sex drive when it gets trapped in the sacral chakra, overthinking when it gets lost in the throat chakra, for example.

The blockages themselves are not a permanent hindrance to the awakened Kundalini's momentum though. If it is sufficiently active, the force will simply burn through the obstacles. This may cause pain on the physical, cognitive, or emotional level depending on what the Kundalini touches. Aside from this, the Kundalini will draw on prana to sustain itself. If the area it finds itself lacks this vital energy, the fire may behave erratically.

Keep in mind that when the awakening process has begun, it is usually unstoppable. It will burn through impediments, cleanse impurities, and untangle knots in the energetic channels. It may influence your energy so that you experience certain events or become predisposed to certain kinds of behavior that will eventually lead to its greater freedom. Thus, you must be willing to face the consequences and do your best to assist its progress.

Consider the Kundalini as an intelligent force that knows what it's doing. Do your best to understand it. If you can't comprehend it, just trust it.

Symptoms of Kundalini Awakening

Kundalini influences the body and mind so its release brings about physical and psychological symptoms. There is a wide range of Kundalini symptoms – some of them highly desirable while others cause frustration.

Body

- Involuntary movements - shaking and jerking
- Involuntary positioning - asanas (Yoga postures) and mudras (Yoga hand gestures
- Unusual sensations - tingling, itching, vibrating, crawling, electric shocks , intense heat or cold, a cool breeze, inner lightness, electric current travelling along the spine or along the arms and hands
- Heightened sensitivity to lights, sounds, bodily sensations
- Restlessness
- Headaches, migraines, pressure, pains
- Increased blood pressure
- Irregular heartbeat
- Disrupted sleep pattern (insomnia or excessive sleeping)
- Disrupted eating pattern (appetite loss or binge eating)
- Disturbed digestive and excretory processes

- Increased strength
- Faster healing
- Greater body-mind coordination
- Strong resistance to illness

Emotions

- A feeling of losing control
- Diminished or increased sexual desire
- Emotional upheavals, mood swings, or numbness
- Intense desire to improve one's self and the world
- Lack of interest in socializing with others
- Bliss
- Tranquility
- Infinite love
- Connection to the universe

Mind

- Changes in perceptions
- Changes in mental function
- Unusual perceptions - visions, sounds, etc.
- Seeing lights in the environment
- Seeing auras or lights around or inside the body (clouds or flashes of colors)
- Altered states of consciousness

- Dissociation
- Depersonalization
- Absorption
- Greater sensitivity to art
- Paranormal experiences: Telepathy, prophetic dreams, visions, hearing disembodied voices and sounds
- Stronger intuition
- Developing new talents, improving old ones
- Ability to make better decisions
- Gaining a direction in life
- Expanded, heightened or deepened awareness
- Transcendent consciousness

Laboratory Measurements

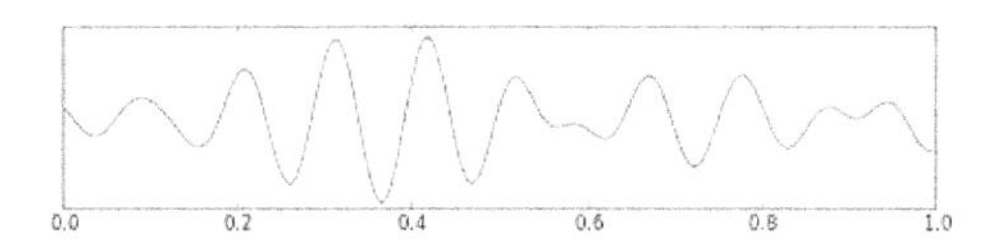

EEG sample showing Alpha waves. Photo by Hugo Gamboa / CC BY

- EEG: Increased alpha or theta waves
- Heart: Decreased heart rate
- Respiration: Decreased respiration rate
- Skin: Increased or decreased skin conductance

(Arambula, 2001)

Intense experiences usually last from 5 to 30 minutes only. Your system will adjust itself to the higher energy level so it will gradually feel normal. If you are overwhelmed by what's happening, reduce your activity levels. Stop exercising and meditating for a while until the symptoms calm down.

These symptoms may be caused by changes in the energy patterns of the individual that is brought about by the ascending Kundalini. Some have theorized that Kundalini awakening is a natural part of human evolution since it causes several changes in a person. According to them, the Kundalini may serve a role in modifying the nervous system to allow the person to function in a different state of existence.

From a study done by Sanchez and Daniels (2008), these symptoms are common among those who practice 'transpersonal activities' – activities that go beyond ordinary personal concerns such as spiritual and mystic practices. These symptoms are not usually present in people who do not perform these kinds of activities.

Also, people who follow different paths may experience different symptoms, with those following 'unstructured paths' (practices that do not prescribe methods) experiencing more unpleasant symptoms than those adhering to 'structured paths' (practices with particular techniques). This means that Kundalini activation is better done intentionally and methodically. Although you can attempt activation on your own, it's best if you can find a teacher who already has an activated Kundalini.

A word of caution: awakening the Kundalini is a serious practice that involves accelerating your spiritual evolution in one lifetime so that you can meet God and attain a god-like state. Sure, it does bring benefits such as better health, psychic abilities, increased magnetism and the likes, but if you are focused on these instead of the process, the activation may not happen. Instead, concentrate on simply doing what you need to in order to activate it. This will give you a pure mindset that's conducive for the activation.

Before anything else, be sincere in determining your reasons for rousing the serpent energy. You must put your whole heart and mind into what you're doing. If you have an internal conflict, a part of you may resist what you're trying to achieve, even to the point that it will create obstacles for you.

Ponder on the things that are truly important to you and determine whether Kundalini activation is in line with that. If not, reflect on what you need to adjust.

If you sense that you're not yet ready, don't rush. The soul has all the time in the Universe. It can patiently wait for one or thousands of lifetimes more, so you don't need to feel pressured into doing it. After all, everything you do down to the most ordinary of actions will contribute to your spiritual growth. You don't really need to dive into mystical practices just because you think you need to or you are just curious about them.

There are times though when the Kundalini stirs even if you're not aware of it or you are not consciously trying to activate it. In this case, it may be a signal that you're being helped with your evolution. If so, it's better if you permit it to happen and cope with the discomfort rather than attempt to stop it.

Chapter 2: What is Kundalini?

Kundalini is known to be the energy of the consciousness that is a spiritual-psycho energy that lives within the resting body, and that is why it needs to be awakened. The term literally means "annular or circular", and was also a name that was often given to snakes in the 12th century.
It originated from the yogic belief that corporeal energy is real and that it resides inside a person's body, particularly at the base of one's spine. Kundalini can be awakened if one connects with his soul and if he decides to seek the truth within himself.
The Kundalini is depicted to represent a sleeping serpent or a goddess at one's spine where all the power and energy comes from. It is also said to be a libidinal or instinctive force.
Kundalini started to get the attention of many in the 1970's, but research has it that a couple of people, including one of the most popular Psychologists in the world, Carl Jung, have known about it even in the early '30's, because they became familiar with Sanskrit and Greek teachings. Incidentally, Kundalini has been used as a technical term in most Shakti or Durga writings even back in the 11th century. It has been used by Yoga Upanishads to show others that they are more powerful than them.

What is it really for?

So, you're probably wondering why you have to awaken Kundali, aren't you? Well, here's what you need to know.

Kundalini is a way of cleansing one's mind and body. In a way, it's like you're detoxifying yourself without actually having to make green juices or changing your diet in a 180 degree manner. Kundali works in such a way that once it is awakened, you can expect it to clean and refresh your body 24 hours a day, seven days a week.

It is also a way of cleansing your chakras, or the parts of your unconscious mind and body that is also known as energy points where vital energy and life forces meet. You will not be able to make the most out of your chakras if you don't awaken your Kundalini.

And, the most important part about awakening Kundalini is that you become whole again—the way that the Supreme Being intended you to be. Because Kundalini is portrayed as a goddess, once it is awakened, it moves toward your head where Lord Shiva, or the Supreme Being resides. So, in a way, you can say that you are now connected to the Supreme Being because you have found a sense of divinity that is not common to most people. God-consciousness, enlightenment, self-realization, and nirvana are just some of the most important things that could happen once Kundalini is awakened.

This way, when time comes that the Supreme Being calls you back to return to Him, you will return as a purified and whole person. Also, because of this, you get to feel a sense of peace that you haven't ever felt before—and which would help you live your life on earth in a more fulfilling manner.

Chapter 3: One Breath at a Time

Learning to meditate can be a little bit like walking into the dark without a flashlight. If you have read or heard people say that have to prevent yourself from thinking about anything, let that go. The idea of meditation is not to block the flow of thoughts, but to channel them, to learn how to not attach to every thought that floats through your mind. It is like going to the market for apples. There are a host of other fruits that look tempting, but you remind yourself that you are only there to buy apples. When thoughts barge their way into your consciousness, you can very nicely say, "No thank you," then return to clarity of your mind. Meditation quietly trains the mind to focus. You learn to concentrate with a clear vision.

Breath awareness is one of the first steps you learn in meditation or any mindful practice such as yoga or tai chi. You are not forcing anything. Rather, you are simply making a conscious choice to not create a story out of thoughts that pass through your mind. You cannot stop thinking, but you can learn to bring your awareness and your attention, to where you want it to go. This process takes time, so be patient with yourself!

There is an interconnectedness to the body, the mind, and the breath. When you bring awareness to your breath, it naturally begins to slow down. And when the breath slows down, the mind and the body relax. Think about when you have been anxious or frightened, your heart pounds, you breath becomes rapid and shallow. When you begin to practice purposeful breathing, meditation becomes easier. It is a preparation for the practice of meditation. Be aware though, even long time meditators sometimes struggle with focus. It is normal to find your mind wandering off, particularly in the beginning.

Meditation is about kindness, you simply repeat to yourself internally to come back to your breath.

To prepare for your meditation session, choose a time that will not be interrupted for at least ten to fifteen minutes. Carving out a set time to meditate and sticking to it (when possible) helps to establish your practice. Early mornings or late evening may be ideal for you, or perhaps you have time in the afternoon that would work. Everyone has unique schedules and circadian rhythms that influence when you sleep, when you are most alert and engaged, or when you are fatigued or have low energy. Choose a time that works for you. Remember, too, it is better to meditate for ten minutes five days a week than to meditate for an hour once a week. Consistency is what helps you establish your new meditation practice.

Where should you meditate? You can practice meditation anywhere, but in the beginning, you want to establish your sweet spot. Try to find a space where you will not be disturbed. The space needs to be a relatively quiet place free of noise that you can control. That said, if you are in your house or apartment and there are children outside playing, dogs barking, etcetera, do not worry. In modern life it is challenging to find a space that is absolutely silent. You just don't want to meditate with a television on, or where there are a lot of distractions, especially in the beginning. During nice weather you may meditate outside, or on a porch or deck. The point to finding a place is again, making it consistent, familiar. When you go to that spot your mind and body recognize it as a place to meditate. It is like doing yoga, when you step on your mat, you step into a place for practice.

If you live in a lively household with a lot of people and finding a space is challenging, there are creative ways around all of that. Try wearing earplugs or headphones. Or, maybe you rise earlier before everyone wakes up in order to get your meditation in. Some people meditate first thing in the morning, which if possible is highly recommended as it can set the tone for the day. If that is not possible, maybe you meditate before going to bed in the evening, letting go of the days events. The crux of meditating is the actual practice, which can literally be done anywhere or any time that you can find where you will not be disturbed. Perhaps the only time you have alone is after work in your office or at lunch. Let those around you know that while you are meditating, you don't want to be disturbed. It is your right to ask for space and time. You are not asking for anything outlandish, remember that. Don't be deterred by people who don't understand your desire for improving the way you navigate through life. It is your life, and meditation will only enhance it.

There is a ritual nature to meditation Think about special holidays you celebrate, whether they are part of a spiritual practice or not. You prepare for them, make particular food or wear certain clothes. Because you are choosing to make it part of your life, a practice with intention, it is good to make preparations. Some people like to build an altar of some sort, others may decorate their meditation space with nature; rocks, or stones, flowers or plants. You may like to light candles or have the lights off. Paying homage to your meditation time and space is another way to honor it, to connect to it and make it important to you.

When you meditate it is important to be able to have your spine straight. Along the vertebrae are nerves that connect to your body; they need to be aligned. Imagine a hose with running water, the water being your energy flow. If you kink that hose or bend it, the flow of water diminishes or stops altogether. You spine is like that hose. Sit on a comfortable chair, making sure your feet touch the ground. Or, sit against a wall (which is great for back support). You can even try lying down. There are also meditation cushions you can buy, but they are not essential to your practice. If you are extremely tired, lying down may be challenging to stay awake. Meditation is not napping, it is a practice in focused attention and as you progress, it will grow in meaning. Wear comfortable clothing that breathe. It is difficult to meditate in tight fitting clothes that cling to you as they impede the breath. In other words, you want to be comfortable when you meditate, and you don't want to be distracted by clothes that are pinching you.

In the beginning, it is best to use a timer. Start with ten to fifteen minutes. A timer will help you relax and you can let go of thinking, "How long have I been meditating?" It is one less thing to distract you. People often ask if it is okay to listen to music while meditating. This will ultimately depend upon the preferences of the individual. If you are playing soft nature tunes such as rain or birds singing or ocean sounds this may help you focus. If possible try to establish a meditation practice that isn't dependent on music though. Some people prefer a soft background of classical music when they meditate. You definitely don't want to play songs with words, unless it is chanting or a soft repetition. If silence is hard to find, put on headphones or wear earplugs to block the noise.

Remember that meditation takes time and practice, much like learning to play an instrument or learning any new skill. The more you do it, the more proficient you become. What is unique about meditation is that the subtle changes will be incremental, and not necessarily overt or obvious. They are internal as opposed to going on a diet and seeing the weight loss when you put on your jeans. It is the consistency of your practice that over time will have a profound and far reaching impact on the quality of your life. Because of the very nature of meditation, in the beginning it may feel like you are not accomplishing anything. It may even feel like you are wasting time. If that happens it is simply the mind looking for excuses. The reptilian aspect of the human brain will want to slip back into what is comfortable, familiar. Let old thoughts pass and practice anyway. All new healthy habits come with a bit of struggle, but soon enough, you will begin to openly look forward to your meditation sessions.

Setting clear goals for when and how long you meditate will help you establish your meditation practice. For example, you commit to setting your alarm for 6 am to meditate for 15 minutes during the week and for 8:30 am on the weekends. Rather than an ambiguous promise to meditate in the morning. Dr. BJ Fogg, a behavioral scientist, found that there are three elements of habit. Cue (triggers, prompts), routine, and reward. Establishing a defined time and place will remove the guesswork. The alarm is your prompt, and the routine will cement your commitment. Then you are rewarded with your progress as you notice a growing sense of mastery over being able to calm down easier, to achieve a subtle serenity, to be present. You can also incorporate milestone rewards, such as treating yourself to a massage after a month of meditation, or whatever feels like a reward to you. Maybe you incorporate a short reading of something that inspires you into your practice over a cup of tea or coffee. Set yourself up for success. Make it a pleasurable experience from the get-go. Pay attention to the particulars, then choose a date to begin and stick to it. There is no room for judgement in meditation. When you start, be easy on yourself, allow room for kindness and acceptance. This practice is new to you, give yourself time.

Chapter 4: Science of the Third Eye

Our third eye is what helps us see the energies and spirits that are hidden amongst the astral plane. In our brains, there is a small endocrine gland called the epiphysis cerebri, or pineal gland. This specific part of our brains is responsible for the production of melatonin, the hormone that is responsible for our state of consciousness, sleep, and also brings along our onset of puberty. This gland is also responsible for our spiritual vision through our mind's eye.

It is believed that our brains are what allow us to see in both the physical and spiritual planes. The pineal gland is considered to be one of the highest sources of light energy that is accessed by humankind. This is also the gland that is responsible for our awakening and initiation of supernatural and spiritual powers. Our third eye is what helps us develop our psychic abilities by giving us a higher vision.

The pineal gland works along with the hypothalamus gland, which is responsible for our more human functions such as hunger, thirst, sexual desire, and even aging. Before the psychic powers of this "third eye" were discovered, it was seen as a mysterious link to the world of superstition and mysticism. One of the most difficult parts of mastering the vision of your mind's eye is being able to trust the information that we are receiving. It can be very difficult to determine the difference between what is spiritual information and what our minds end up creating in their experience.

It is said that activation of our third eye will feel like a deep pressure at the center or base of our brain. This center is responsible for the awakening of our mind's eye, also considered as our sixth chakra, Ajna. Our pineal gland has also been referred to as "the principal seat of the soul," and opens the portal in our minds to the higher dimensions energies of the Divine.

The pineal gland is also surprisingly responsible for the development of DMT within our brains. It is said that DMT is what is released from this gland during near-death experiences, allowing the individual to have higher spiritual visions and awakenings. Our third eye is what is responsible for our ability to have higher wisdom and awareness, which in turn will bring spiritual visions.

To be able to access the power of our pineal gland, it is critical to focus on freeing the sixth chakra of any blockages and rid the brain of harmful toxins. If we allow our brains to become susceptible to these toxins, the blocks in our Nadi will only intensify. Many things can lead to the poisoning of our pineal gland, ranging from poor diet, anxiety, and stress from our daily trials.

There are also many chemicals that the human body ingests daily that will also lead to a weakened pineal gland. One of these toxins is fluoride, which is used in almost all toothpaste and even tap waters. Foods that have been contaminated with pesticides and humanmade preservatives will also negatively affect our pineal gland, causing it to grow even more sluggish and weak.

A full body detox would be very wise to do in the process of decalcifying our mind's eye. The pineal gland was initially believed to be the size of a lemon, but today, the normal gland would be the size of a pea. Poor diet and lifestyles have caused the pineal gland to slowly shrink over time, weakening it tremendously in the process. We can bring back strength to this part of our brains by making sure to rid the toxins from our diet while also being sure to gain lots of supplemental calcium.

This change can be rather strict, removing or limiting our intake of sugar, caffeine, alcohol, and tobacco. We can help the healing process of our brains and strengthen our pineal glands by ingesting lots of pure water and switching to organic foods. Taking raw apple cider vinegar and 100% pure cacao have incredibly positive effects on the pineal gland too.

Once our pineal has been entirely rid of toxins, activation of our third eye can be promoted through meditation and direct sunlight. The practice of Surya Yoga was often used by the Great Himalayan Masters, which involved gazing into the sun. Staring into the rising sun was one of the best ways to practice this, as dawn is when the earth's magnetic field is charged. While light is vital for the awakening of our third eye, it is also essential to make sure that we sleep in complete darkness. This darkness allows our bodies to completely shut down and rest, releasing more melatonin and serotonin that helps promote healthy pineal growth.

Our third eyes are responsible for detecting the vibrational energies around us and putting them into a visual form for us to perceive. These energies can be seen as either colorful auras or in the forms of spiritual beings. Many have even reported being able to have visions and even conversations with those who have passed.

The awakening and healing of our third eye can excel through the use of specially designed music that reverberates specific vibrations that react with and heal our pineal gland. The use of healing music in our meditations is highly recommended, as the additional vibrations will help activate specific points in our chakra that will allow us to heal. It is possible to heal our mind and bring peace back to our daily thoughts, and opening our third eyes is just the first step in becoming powerful enough to go beyond our physical being and achieve astral projection.

It is also important to realize that not all spiritual signs and messages will be communicated verbally, but may show up in our lives through material items that hold significance to a particular individual. For example, many report the appearance of items, music, letters, human speech, or even numbers. If we are open to the messages of these spirits who are trying to connect, these certain happenings will stand out and resonate with us.

We control our ability to activate our third eye and open our senses to those that dwell in the astral plane. If we do not want to receive any communication with these spirits or entities, we can cut any connection. Those of us who may not be ready for a spiritual awakening might be frightened from suddenly hearing or seeing those who have already passed on. There is no need to fear for we are perfectly capable of ridding ourselves of any harmful attachments, or even merely, temporarily delay communication through the astral plane until we are ready.

We may ask those who are trying to communicate to try a different approach if we are not ready to completely connect, as there are many tools available that can help us communicate in very safe and healthy ways. Tarot cards, pendulums, and rune stones are just a few talismans that can help us experiment with communication of the other side without taking such a drastic leap into unfamiliar territory.

There are others who are much more open to the awakening of their third eye and readily leap into the journey of spiritual awakening through the help of those from higher planes. We can naturally detect whether an entity is either positive or negative and easily continue or cut off any further connection. No matter how hard some negativity may try to lead us astray or even frighten us, there is no need to fear.

Using white sage frequently to clear our home and our stones of negative vibrations is a practice that is highly recommended. This powerful gift of mother earth will repel all negativity from our environment and our auric field so that only positivity may dwell in its place. Through this, we can guarantee that our meditation and third eye healing and awakening will be promoted only by influences of positivity.

The practice of awakening our mind's eye is another ability that will require a lot of patience, but the results are worth it. To be able to make contact in or to travel through the Astral Plane is something that all Gurus have practiced at one point in their lives.

Another excellent tool for vibrational energies is the Tibetan singing bowl. These are small bells that are usually in the shape of bowls. When struck with their provided mallet, the singing bowls erupt with sound and resonate deep vibrations that channel directly into our Nadi. The vibrational waves from the bowl are excellent for cleansing our auras and grounding our minds. The beautiful song that emanates from these instruments can be heard and felt on a spiritual level that can influence the progress of our spiritual healing and awakening.

It is almost guaranteed for these singing bowls to help activate the uncoiling of Kundalini while also helping break away the blocked passages that stand in our Divine Mother's way.

There are many ways to experiment with the vibrations of the universe and the effects they have on our auric field, so taking the time to research and find the right tools for our awakening are essential.

Some people are also known to use Divining Rods to try to communicate with the vibrations from the Astral Plane. These sensory rods will pick up the magnetic energy and waves around them that will in turn influence the direction of their swing. It is crucial to make sure that we have grounded our energies before using these types of tools and talismans because our vibrational waves can influence them as well.

Many different machines have been made as well, that do not mainly help with the awakening of our Kundalini but help detect the variations of energy and vibrations in the surrounding environment to communicate with those from the Astral Plane.

Usually, these types of devices are frequently in use for many famous paranormal investigational shows.

Some tools will even offer an excess amount of energy for surrounding spirits and entities to draw from to give them enough power to be able to communicate through voice, touch, or even visual manifestation.

Children are known for almost always being able to detect and visually see being from the Astral Plane. When we are so new to this world, the veils that first cover our eyes are not fully developed. Children are such pure forms of innocent energy, and this innocence remains untouched for most of our early lives. There are many reports of children interacting with individuals who are not necessarily there. The reason for this is that the pineal gland is still healthy and undeterred by the toxins of this plane that hinder its ability to connect us with vibrational energies from the other side.

Many children will also almost always have incredibly vivid dreams of travel and flight, which usually is their astral projection that is still excitedly exploring the universe around it. Time can and will add layers to our energies, slowly burying our spiritual abilities until we actively help to decalcify them.

Children often will hold knowledge that a lot of us will lack regarding the Astral Plane. These pure souls hold more power and wisdom than most of us will usually give them credit. Many Gurus dedicate their lives to restoring the pineal gland to its original glory and returning to the higher sense of spirituality that we once held as children.

Of course, every one of us still holds this Divine power, but it can become buried and hidden away after the trials of life pile on top of our spiritual energy. We never honestly lose our Divine capabilities, but it is imperative to the progress of our health that we try to strengthen our powers further, reinforcing our mighty armory of vibrational influences.

Many beings might not have as much faith in the power and abilities of younger humans, but this does not mean that these powers do not exist. The harsh lessons of life will fog our spiritual sight and drive us further away from our true awakening.

The pools of energy that make up our auric field will never cease to exist, but their flow of power can and will be hindered by life's many challenges. By understanding the causes of our everyday trials and the effect they have on our auric field, we can more successfully battle these blocks.

Awakenings in our third eye will also allow us to detect forms from the ethereal plane through our everyday human vision as well. Many times these sightings will be reported as orbs of light, color, or even full body apparitions that appear in the peripheral vision and disappear once we try to look at them directly. These psychic visual powers that we possess can be developed by many different practices, a lot of which are Kundalini exercises.

Being able to focus on this spiritual vision is ironically achieved by relaxing and blurring our eyes. It is an excellent practice to use visual illusion books to train this sense of sight, as they reveal hidden images that can only be seen after extensively relaxing the eyes. Mastering this vision does not mean that any time we relax our eyes dozens of forms will pop up before us. Psychic vision and the awakening of our third eye will take dedication and time, allowing us to see only those who dwell on the Astral Plane.

Awakening the power of our Kundalini will significantly help us excel in our psychic abilities, allowing us to help build on our confidence to explore the Fifth Plane. It is imperative that we work to enhance every one of our spiritual abilities so that we may excel in opening the paths of our Nadi and calling on the wisdom of our Kundalini.

These spiritual practices are almost always universal, and all tie together with the same goal of reaching a higher state of being and peace of mind. There is no higher proof than that provided to us from the many creeds and lands that harnessed the power of the Divine energies of the earth to help them grow mentally and spiritually.

Native American practices frequently used the cleansing powers of sage and called upon the powers of the earth, learning their spiritual ways from the wise teachings provided by nature. Many sacred Native American chants are combined with powerful drumming to resonate with our vibrational energy. This form of vibrational influence is very similar to the practice of mantras in almost all Kundalini exercises. It is in Native American teachings that vibrations from the wings of a hummingbird emanate the song of pure joy and illumination, awakening the medicine flowers and opening our hearts.

Even Christianity uses the mighty power of song and vibrational energies through the beautiful Gregorian Chants. These chants are used in Christian meditational practices around the world, allowing those who listen to clear their minds and focus their vibrational waves and energies. Some churches are explicitly architecturally designed to enhance these waves of vibration to enhance the spiritual power that they provide.

These vocal powers of vibration are not exclusive to humans, as there are many species of animals that not only use vibrational waves for healing and communication but some, such as bats, will use these vibrations as a way of detecting that which is surrounding their environment. Using our abilities in a similar form of echolocation, we can use the power of vibrational waves to detect variances in our astral environment.

Chapter 5: How To Awaken a Dormant Kundalini

Close your eyes and take a deep breath. Try to quiet your mind from any thoughts. What do you feel at this point? One of the things that could have crossed your mind is your pulse. If things were really quiet, you might just hear a slight buzzing which is the energy coursing through your veins and encompassing your muscles and enveloping your whole body. If you felt this way but don't really know what it is or can't put a finger on a name, well then this most likely is kundalini.

By now, we know that Kundalini is a universally acknowledged and revered energy that exists in our lives. This coiled energy is awakened through Kundalini yoga, and those who practice it and subsequently release the coiled serpent from its slumber is said to receive spiritual enlightenment and a heightened sense of conscious awareness. Below, you can see the energy flow through the chakras when this dormant energy is released and freed. Those who awaken Kundalini energy are said to be more creative, more inspired and balanced in spirituality, mentality, and mind. Since Kundalini is considered the life force that ignites everyday function of our minds as well as our bodies it makes sense that we need to unlock this energy as it will only help us unveil our true potential as well as our creativity.

What's Yoga Got to Do with Kundalini?

Yoga was originally used as a path to enlightenment, but with more and more practitioners gravitating towards yoga as a stress and anxiety reliever, the spiritual aspect of yoga was not fully embraced.

For those actually seeking out the spiritual practice of yoga, this is where Kundalini is used as the yoga of choice. Instead of focusing on just the spirit or just the body or just the mind, kundalini yoga incorporates all these three elements into one holistic process that leads towards the release of energy. With regards to the physical aspect of the practice, kundalini yoga focuses on deriving the energy meridians or points where the energy flow is the best to heighten the awareness and to activate specific areas such as the spine and the navel. Key breathing techniques are also vital such as the pranayama that assists practitioners to control their breathing and unlocking their energy within. These physical attributes are done to achieve a higher state of awareness.

How to Awaken a Dormant Kundalini

Kundalini energy can be dormant for many reasons or for no reasons at all. Just as how it comes to you, it can also leave. So how do you awaken a dormant kundalini? If you want to discover and awaken kundalini, here are 15 ways you can do that to facilitate and create progress in your practice:

1.Focus Your Breath

Breathing is one of the vital aspects of yoga practice of any kind. You may have gone off course with your breathing, and it could be that you got distracted. To get back on track is to do the most basic elements in kundalini practice which is to control your breathing. Focus on breathing towards the tail of your spine and then directing it upwards towards the crown of your head.

2. Focus on your posture

You are most likely sitting at least 70% of your waking hours, and this only leads to bad posture because we are sitting in the car, we are sitting in the office, we are sitting in meetings, and all of this makes us hunch or walk differently or sit wrongly and even sleep wrongly. Bad posture also prevents us from breathing properly which is why in yoga practice, yogis and gurus always start a pose by telling to sit tall and keep our spine stacked.

3. Reject Negativity

Staying positive will help us to improve and also keeps us objective and looking forward to our goals and tasks at hand. By focusing on the positive aspects of our daily lives, we reject negativity and develop wholesomely in both our practice, our spirituality, and mentality.

4. Refine Your Diet

If you are trying to awaken your internal energy, then we need to look at our practice holistically. Standing right, breathing right and staying positive also includes eating right and this means eating wholesome and healthy meals. Kundalini awakening also requires us to eat less meat. Over time, those practicing for years eventually eliminate meat from their diet. This is not a must, but it is encouraged. Eating the right foods helps keep you in a healthy mindset and gives your mood an overall good complex.

5. Move Your Body

You can move your body in various ways such as doing exercise, being one with nature, and doing physical work. Ideally, you want to move your body through the exercise that you enjoy so this can be anything like long walks or bicycling or even jogging. Your body needs the movement which is why yoga also incorporates asanas to pull, elongate strength and warm the body. There is no good keeping the body sedentary.

6. Stay Strong

It is good to stay strong, but it is also good to accept and understand that not everything is within your will and control. There will be days that things will go absolutely amazing while there are days that things will go bad and there are days that are just ok. Life is that way but in moments of adversity, staying strong mentally helps you get through the darkest moments.

7. Find Your Circle

Birds of a feather do flock together. We, subconsciously, mirror the people we are surrounded by and people we grew up with. Some of us having a pretty positive surrounding while some of us do not. The good thing is as we grow up, we can choose and create this surrounding by ourselves. We can consciously make decisions to surround ourselves with the people we want to be like, and this can be the kindest or the most honest, or the most successful. Our quality of life entirely depends on who we choose to be around with to attain our goals.

8. Get a Mentor

A yogi mentor is an excellent person to surround yourself with. You can have a deeper connection with your yogi and also learn from them and share your Kundalini experiences with each other. Part of this mentorship is also ensuring that you have the right kind of support from someone who has experience.

9. Chant, Chant, Chant

Yogis rarely practice in silence. They usually chant and repeat mantras as it is a way of facilitating the Kundalini mood. Chanting is a great devotional practice to get your dormant Kundalini to revive itself and uncoil its energy. Join a group or find a teacher that you are comfortable with and repeats chants to help you rekindle the energy within you.

10. Activate Your Interests

In this busy and hectic lifestyle, we live in it is easy to get caught up and do only tasks and things that we feel we should not because we like it but because we think it's the right thing to do, or because it is expected of us or because we should do it. All this may deactivate the energy within you. To reignite it again, set aside an hour each day for yourself to pursue the tasks and things that you feel connects you back to your inner soul. Make this one hour an hour of your enjoyment.

11. Be here and be now

Be present to the situation and surroundings that your body is currently in as you go throughout the day. We need to be conscious of our surroundings and not to get caught up in a daze. Direct your focus by cutting out your extraneous thinking and instead live in the moment at hand. Mindfulness is what would also help revive a dormant kundalini and leave you feeling more grounded and satisfied.

12. Go with The Flow

Going with the flow is ideal especially if you have been organizing your life to minute detail. Sometimes it is great to just let go and get rid of intense planning and instead, take each day as it comes. View your day as an adventure as opposed to a planned battle. If your day does not go as expected, keep positive and know that not everything is within your control.

13. Affirmations

While we are nice and accommodating to the people around us, rarely are we kind to ourselves. Rarely do we take the time to take care of us because who else will? When we are always looking out for other people and not ourselves, our kundalini energy also suffers Take time out from your schedule to remind yourself of how beautiful life is, the things you are grateful for as well as your talents and attributes.

14. Cut Distractions

We often seek things that numb us such as binge-watching TV or browsing the internet or only looking at our cell phones. When our spirit has lost its direction, our energy also loses its compass. To awake the dormant kundalini, you can also start by not engaging with the people around you. You can switch off gadgets after 7 pm and only focus on yourself and your family. You can also distant yourself away from certain people for a certain period of time. Whatever you do, make a commitment to yourself that you want to eliminate distractions.

15. Try using music for relaxation

When you get into your asanas and meditations, putting on a flowing rhythm and music will promote your senses to get into a meditative state and assist in your kundalini awakening. At the end of the day, you do not want to rush and wake up a dormant kundalini overnight. Spiritual enlightenment is a gradual process of learning, healing, stepping back and understanding what it takes and how to get there. Kundalini is a practice, and it does not happen overnight. So be mindful of what you can do within a certain period and keep progressing from there.

Chapter 6: Seven Main Chakras

The First Chakra - Muladhara Chakra

Located almost at the very end of the spine and touching the anus and testicles or cervix, this chakra is designated as the four-petalled lotus, whose petals represent ultimate happiness, innate bliss, the bliss of unity and bliss of courage and strength. She is considered a reflection of the crown chakra on the physical level, and therefore her petals are blissful. The nature of this chakra is identical to Brahman, the creative principle of the universe. We can assume that it preserves the material form of the body and that its underlying history and potentials of human evolution are hidden.

This is the foundation and support of the body, and its safety and self-preservation depend on its normal functioning. This chakra corresponds to the element earth, orange-red color, and sense of smell. An elephant with a black stripe around the neck is its symbol and represents earthly qualities: strength, firmness, stability and support, these qualities are represented by the yellow square inscribed in the circle of yantra or mandala depicting this chakra. It also has a triangle called Tripura and represents will, knowledge, and action.

Muladhara affects the rectum, kidneys, sperm accumulation, and the genitals, as well as bones, skin, muscles, nerves, and hair. It is associated with the occurrence of physiological disorders such as hemorrhoids, constipation, sciatica, and prostate diseases. It is associated with a sense of smell, and its vibration causes expansion or contraction of the lungs.

Mishra writes that through pratyahara (distraction of the senses), anger, lust, and greed are curbed on this chakra. Longing and depression are also considered symptoms of an imbalance in it.

Meditation on this chakra establishes control over attachments to luxury, lies, pride, envy, and narcissism. Pandit said that the Muladhara controls physical or subconscious movements or impulses. In the yantra (the symbolic image of the chakra), there is a blood-red triangle of fire that inflates the kandarpa vayu, the cause of sexual arousal, which is important for reproducing the human race. Motoyama wrote that when this chakra awakens, it releases suppressed emotions explosively, which can lead to the emergence of extreme irritability and psychological instability in a person, a violation of sleep patterns, excitability.

Meditation on the god of this chakra, Mahadeva, who sits with his face, turned back, cleanses from sins. Brahma, the god of absolute creative power, also gives this chakra the goddess Dakini Shakti, the energy of creation. If you repeat the mul mantra, while maintaining the serenity of the mind and devotion and focusing on this chakra, then you can awaken her goddess. In yoga cosmology, exactly under this chakra is the Kundalini energy, curled up in three and a half turns. Yogis believe that this is where the confluence of sushumna (nadi, carrying the stream of life), Vajra Nadi (nadi carrying the electric stream), and Brahma Nadi (sound stream or stream of spirit) merge.

The Second Chakra - Svadhishthana Chakra

Located slightly above the muladhara at the base of the penis, or in the center of the lower back, this chakra is associated with the conquest of water; its symbols are the crescent and the god Vishnu, nourishing the principle of the universe. Its color is usually considered red or scarlet and sometimes - white. Rakini Shakti, a dark blue goddess with three red eyes and four hands, from whose nose blood flows, carries the energy of this chakra. She holds in her hands a trident, a lotus, a drum, and a chisel. A light gray or green sea monster resembling a crocodile is an animal symbol of the chakra, it personifies dominance over the sea and indicates a connection with the unconscious. By meditating on this chakra, a person defeats the elements.

She has six petals, which represent the mental qualities of neglect, numbness, credulity, suspicion, desire for destruction and cruelty, and also represent six nerves associated with the colon, rectum, kidneys, bladder, genitals, and testicles. This chakra promotes the circulation of liquid substances in the body, their conservation, and nutrition; it is also considered a center of the heterosexual orientation of a person.

Mishra wrote that this chakra controls, controls, and nourishes the feet. By focusing on it, a person feels a magnetic pulsation, circulation, and vibration and can get rid of all the unpleasant sensations, pains, and illnesses in his legs. Other conditions associated with this chakra include sexual problems, diabetes, kidney and bladder diseases. By meditating on it, a person is freed from egoistic feelings, small impulses, and desires. The equanimity and serenity of the mind develop. The normal functioning of the Svadhishthana is associated with a sense of self-confidence and well-being, and with the frustrations in her work, disappointment, addiction, and anxiety. This chakra is also associated with a sense of taste and language. According to some tantras, in order to master it, a person must master the language.

The Third Chakra - Manipura Chakra

Located above Svadvishthana opposite the navel, Manipura is associated with Rudra, a god who distributes goods and creates fear, personifying the destructive principle of the universe (the world of the mind). The goddess Lakini Shakti, dressed in yellow clothes, is called the benefactress of the universe, and one of the texts describes that she loves animal meat, her chest is covered with blood, and fat is dripping from her lips. The animal symbol is a ram, an animal sacrificed, which personifies the need to sacrifice addictions, impulsive urges, and other strong emotions.

Concentration over manipura brings comprehension of feces or eternal time. Perhaps this level of openness can be associated with the return of memories of other lives or states that take people beyond the boundaries of consciousness created by time. This chakra is also associated with control of heat and directs the agni, the fiery principle, which is believed to control the creature's unbridled movements and digestive system. Manipura controls the internal organs of the abdomen, in particular, the functioning of the stomach, liver, and large intestine, and is associated with a section of the central nervous system located above the lumbar region. Some say that focusing on this center can cure diseases of the abdominal organs, especially if you meditate on the red color in it.

Ten petals that carry the qualities of shame, treachery, envy, desire, drowsiness, despondency, vainness, delusion, disgust, and fear make up this chakra. However, according to one of the tantric texts, when a yogi meditates on this chakra and pronounces a mul mantra, he is always in a good mood and illnesses cannot penetrate his / her body. Such a yogi can enter into the bodies of others and see siddhas (saints and teachers of yoga), can, at a glance, determine the qualities of material objects and see objects underground. It is clear why this chakra is so often associated with gaining power and finding a good place in the world. It is also an area of hara that one focuses on during some Zen meditations. This concentration gives rise to a sense of stability and resilience in the being,

The opening of this chakra requires the participation of the eyes and such control over their movements so that they do not for a moment come off the center located between the eyebrows.

The Fourth Chakra - Anahata Chakra

The location of the heart chakra is usually indicated opposite the center line running between the nipples, but sometimes it is moved slightly to the right of the sternum, although not directly above the heart. It is associated with the conquest of the element of air, as well as with the heart and nada, the sound of cosmic consciousness. By meditating on this center, you can feel how the energy flows throughout the entire nervous system as if it is filled with magnetism. Many traditions of spiritual development emphasize the importance of the heart chakra as the chakra that needs to be awakened in the first place in order to experience a spiritual awakening since it is here that the energies of the lower and upper levels of consciousness merge, which symbolize two intersecting triangles. In addition, anahata, combining the energies of different chakras, also connects the left and right sides of the body, the qualities of yin and yang.

Isha is the god of this chakra; he sits on a black antelope or gazelle, which symbolizes the speed and ease of air. Isha is the supreme God, endowed with complete yogic power, omniscient, and omnipresent. It is white and symbolizes purity; it has three eyes; the third represents knowledge of samadhi. When its form arises during meditation, fears disappear, and concentration intensifies.

The yantra images of the heart chakra include intersecting triangles, inside which are a bright golden creature and Kakini Shakti, the lightning-colored goddess who radiates light and joy. Kakini is called the keeper of the doors of Anahata and meditating on it; a person learns to stabilize prana and remove obstacles on the way to Isha. When the goddess is red, it means that her power is used to control pranic energy; when she is white, she is Isha consciousness.

The twelve scarlet petals associated with Anahata represent waiting, excitement, diligence, affection, hypocrisy, weakness, selfishness, separation, greed, fraud, indecision, and regret. Meditation on this chakra brings possession of sound, and if you say the mul mantra during meditation, you are more prepared to understand God, as a person gains control over his feelings, in particular, reducing the sense of touch. Then, as they say, not a single desire will remain unfulfilled - then a person will forever plunge into a state of bliss.

If you look from a different point of view, we can assume that, freed from attachment to all "heart" desires (as evidenced by the qualities embodied in the petals), a person gains the ability to distract the senses from all worldly things and thus acquire a state of bliss first for short periods and then forever.

The qualities of compassion, acceptance, and unconditional love are signs of the balanced functioning of this chakra. Indifference, passivity, and sadness are signs of an imbalance — some authors associate arthritis and respiratory problems with cardiac chakra, as well as cardiovascular disease and hypertension.

The opening of this chakra is considered feasible with the help of the skin; that is, you need to surpass the sense of touch, which is done by achieving control over sensory perception through kumbhaka (breath-holding). A common way to discover the energy of anahata is a meditation on it with the simultaneous presentation of light or breathing in and breathing out air from it.

The Fifth Chakra - Vishuddha Chakra

Located in the throat is the vishuddhi lotus - gray or silver (and sometimes smoky purple) and has sixteen petals. They contain seven musical notes, poison and nectar, and seven "invocations," which are used to protect against demons, during sacrifices, to light sacred lights, to give determination, to bless and glorify. Here begin the priestly or occult powers associated with the forces of projection or expression. This chakra is also associated with the conquest of the etheric state of matter (space). This chakra is usually associated with creative activity and inspiration, as well as receiving moral instruction, especially when in contact with an inexhaustible source of "grace." A person begins to feel that the inner giver and taker are one and the same.

The god of this chakra is Shiva in a half male, half female form (Ardhanarishvara), he sits on a white elephant, and with him is the four-armed yellow Shakini Shakti (goddess). He owns a variety of knowledge. She rules in the kingdom of the moon over insignificant secrets.

Vishuddha controls both hands and is the center of pratyahara or distraction of the senses. When a person focuses attention here, he loses his hands sensitivity to heat, cold, pain, pressure, touch, and temperature. Tantras say that the instruments of this chakra are ears, they are used in such a way that the noise of the world does not distract, and only one sound is heard: either nada (the sound of Ohms is of less intensity) or the name of God. Meditation on this chakra leads one to the threshold of great liberation.

The Sixth Chakra - Ajna Chakra

Ajna is located above the nose between the eyebrows is the source of two nerve flows, one of which passes through the eyes, and the other through the midbrain. There are three main nadi (sushumna, ida, and pingala). The ability to create and achieve is generated by mental waves emanating from this point. This chakra controls the inner vision and dynamic activity of the will and knowledge. This "third eye" in many cultures is associated with light, inner knowledge, intuition, and mediumistic abilities. The discovery of these abilities involves the integration of both intellectual and emotional poles.

The goddess of ajna is the six-faced and six-armed Hakini Shakti; she personifies the five principles concentrated in the lower chakras and the gifts of the ajna chakra. When its color is described as red, then the knowledge of Kundalini is fully awakened; when she is white, she represents a state of rest;

when it is dark blue, it is on the verge of transitioning into a shapeless state. When seen in a combination of white, red, and black colors, she shows a mixture of three gunas: sattva (harmonious consciousness), rajas (activity) and tamas (inertia).

Meditation on this center brings visions of the highest truth, yogic powers, liberation from all Sanskars, and ultimately wisdom, higher knowledge. This is the center of individual consciousness, which through pratyahara, can be expanded to universal. Ajna is often referred to as guiding all other chakras, and some yogis advise to concentrate only on it, or first of all, before awakening energies in other centers. Thus, the development of the qualities inherent in all previous chakras can be influenced, and so the student can achieve a state of nondual consciousness. It is believed that it is not possible to fully master the lower chakras before Ajna is awakened.

The Seventh Chakra - Sahasrara Chakra

According to some texts, sahasrara is located at the top of the head in the brain; others believe that it is above the physical body and is identical with Parabrahma, the supreme creator. Her lotus has a thousand petals, five of which represent all the letters of the Sanskrit alphabet. Samadhi, felt through this chakra, is a complete merger with existence, without the limits of ego-consciousness in the body. (Although there are yoga systems in which other levels of chakras are indicated, extending further beyond the physical body and to this first level of higher consciousness.)

Parabrahma governs this center, symbolized by the triangle of consciousness, which is called Vija - this is another name for the divine essence of sat-chit-ananda. It represents overcoming obstacles and merging with emptiness or the Upper Light outside the form, a state which, according to most yogic sacred books and the saying of the saints, a person cannot describe.

Meditating here, according to Bose and Haldor, a person crosses the boundaries of creation, preservation, and destruction and can taste the sweet nectar (amrita) flowing in a continuous stream from sahasrara. A person is freed, all Sanskars are destroyed, and then he is not subject to either birth or death. At this stage of awakening, individual identification disappears forever, and a person is identified with a higher consciousness. (It is important to remember that when yogis talk about the state of immortality, they usually do not mean that a person will literally never leave the body, but rather imply that conscious fusion with the infinite is achieved forever and will not be destroyed with the death of the body.)

Chapter 7: How To Meditate Effectively

Now that you want to begin practicing meditation, you have to consider how to do it as effectively as possible. This section will help you learn how you can practice meditation in an effective way.

Begin Slowly

Keep in mind to not get sucked into some of the meditation strategies that are out there. Some of them will require you to sit for long hours on end, while others may have a series of directions on how you carry out breathing amid meditation, on how you sit in a particular position and a big heap of stuff that is, at its core, insignificant. When you are an apprentice at meditation, you should try to begin this practice slowly. Rather than instantly hopping into longer meditations, begin with sitting alone without anyone to disturb you for around 5 minutes every day. Following a few weeks of doing this, try to stretch the time out to 10 minutes. Keep adding to your meditation time when you think you can. Try not to push yourself too much because the length of the time doesn't make a difference. It's how consistently committed you are to this training. This is the thing that truly matters.

It's Simple

In the event that it feels too difficult, you are probably not doing it right. You may be trying to force yourself to stop all your thoughts or being too hard on yourself. Try not to give yourself a chance to become too obsessed with the subtleties of the meditation technique. There is no ideal space, time, or ideal perspective that you have to adhere to in order to meditate properly. These things are just minor details that don't matter in the big picture. When you meditate, it should feel simple and normal, regardless of whether it means sitting quietly while you are using your computer, or just driving in your vehicle.

Adhere to a Particular Method

Don't fixate on using the correct meditation method and keep shifting things around, trying new techniques each and every day. Maybe just pick one technique you can identify with and stick to it regardless of anything else. Pursue that technique persistently for a month if you want it to begin working for you.

Be Kind to Yourself First

This ought to be your mantra for all your life. It's one of the most important rules to remember when you are doing anything, including meditation. Meditation is for you to realign your vitality and enable the energy to flow effectively through your mind and body. You have to make peace with where you are as opposed to constantly beating yourself up about where you should have been. The same applies to your meditation practice. In the event that you avoid your meditation session for a day or two, be forgiving to yourself and have the persistence to proceed with the meditation the next day. Missing a day of meditation is not something to worry too much about, just don't make it a habit.

Practice Patience

For our entire lives, we put so much pressure on ourselves to be the ideal version of ourselves, only to later realize that flawlessness is essentially a myth. Meditation is intended to get rid of such pressure from our lives. In the event that you are on a journey to achieve perfection even while meditating, I ask you this: What's the point? The point of consistently meditating is to give yourself a break while trying to achieve a sense of harmony between your brain and body. Practice self-compassion without constraining yourself to meditate at a specific time or spot. Just be patient with yourself.

Don't be Judgmental

Try not to pass judgment on anybody in your life and above all else, don't pass judgment on yourself. Nothing is set in stone. Everybody has the free will to live their lives in the manner in which they choose to, and there's no compelling reason to characterize something as bad and good or wrong and right. When you let go of such judgment, you will find that it is easy to meditate. Meditation is tied in with removing your protective barrier from all the negative events throughout your life, so you can have a better experience later on. In order to do that, you should be in a space where you are totally non- judgmental about everything in your daily life.

Set a Morning Schedule

Once again I repeat: don't be excessively hard on yourself while you do this. While meditation can be performed at pretty much any time, a morning schedule will surely be progressively effective to guarantee that your day goes well. Making it a point to meditate for a couple of minutes each and every morning will allow you to have superior control on your feelings and basic capacity to make decisions for the rest of the day. Additionally, it's simpler to persuade yourself to stick to something amid the beginning of the day than it is at the end of a monotonous day.

Utilize Guided Meditations

Guided meditations work very well for those who have just begun meditation. As a first timer, when you first begin meditation, you may find meditation techniques a little difficult. Guided meditations are fundamentally just soundtracks intended to guide you through each phase of meditation. It's valuable for people who need assistance during their meditation sessions. The best part about these audio files is that for the most part, they are totally free and you can easily find a lot of them on the Internet. With the assistance of guided meditation, you won't need to stress over what to do right away. You can just unwind while adhering to the directions being given to you via these audio files.

Get a Meditation Buddy

Doesn't everything get simpler when having a companion with you? You can get yourself a meditation partner and share the experience together. Being accountable to someone for your meditation practice is a great way to remain persistent. Following each other's advancement, sharing positive thoughts or helping each other remain centered can go far in guaranteeing that you practice meditation as a lifestyle. As people, we are bound to stick to something when we have made a promise to somebody that we will do so.

Find a Meditation Support Group

Can't find a mate to meditate with? Join a support group. These gatherings include a lot of individuals who have dedicated themselves to meditation. Here, you won't just discover individuals who can spur you on, but you will also have a huge gathering of individuals supporting you at whatever point you may stumble off track. Making meditation a habit may not come easy to many of us, and mindfulness groups can allow us to accomplish our meditative goals.

Chapter 8: Kundalini Awakening

This chapter is dedicated to those readers who are ready to work directly on kundalini awakening. In the subsequent pages, you will find 29 techniques to help your kundalini awakening along, and the chapter ends with 6 additional methods that you can try to boost your experience. Whether you've felt kundalini awakening before or you just learned about it for the first time through this book, the tips included in this chapter are guaranteed to provide substance, depth, and insight into your experiences as you proceed.

Awakening Techniques

Ranging from meditation techniques to interpersonal tips and simple world navigation tactics, the options provided in this section will help you move past simple knowledge of kundalini and awakening to the place where knowledge can be put into practice. Gather your yoga mat, your incense, and your mind, for things are about to get amplified.

Apply Kundalini Yoga to Your Practice

The more that you're able to do so, adding physical layers to your meditative practice will be incredibly beneficial. Kundalini yoga is the best place to start, especially if you're working on kundalini awakening in particular, rather than just awareness or chakra balancing. Kundalini yoga will help you work through those chakra blockages and get the kundalini going while boosting your meditative practice within the dimension of the moving human body. You'll be surprised how well it all works together once you start amplifying your practice with yoga.

Use Visualization Techniques to Increase Shakti Movement

Visualization is almost essential to use as a means of increasing shakti movement throughout your body in the form of your kundalini. The ancient Indians were on the right page when they gave relatable names to these cosmic wells of energy within us. They understood how powerful metaphor and imagery can be when it comes to the workings of the inner body (and one's subtle energy). For example, as a reminder, "kundalini" means little coiled one–the snake of universe or source energy (shakti) that exists at the base of our spine. We are meant to imagine this snake being charmed and winding its way through our chakras. We are meant to visualize this and many more things. The more visualization you can incorporate into your practice, the better.

Use Guided Meditation Techniques to Increase Shakti Movement

A lot of people need help detaching from the distractions of the mind and the world before they can focus enough to visualize these intricate inner movements. In this cases, I always recommend guided meditation. There are so many ways to help raise your kundalini based on the techniques people share on online meditation forums and even on sites like YouTube. Audio books of guided meditations could also provide the guidance you'll need to be able to shut off that conscious brain and simply, meditatively focus on the shakti–that pure and potent source energy that wants to move within you. Seek out these guided meditations for kundalini awakening, and you'll be so grateful you did.

Try Pulling the Kundalini Up from Your Crown

This technique, in terms of an awakening booster, is a little more detail-oriented than some others. It comes to the way you visualize the kundalini moving from that spinal source within you to the tip of your crown and back down. Essentially, you'll want to try shifting your focus. If you've been imagining things (as most of us will innately do) as if the serpent has been rising up from your base–with that root chakra as your energetic center from which it leaves and to which it eventually returns–switch things up in an impactful yet subtle way. Imagine your crown chakra as your energetic center and see the kundalini being pulled up through your body, as if drawn by a magnet that rests at the top of your head. Then, once the kundalini rises to this crown point, imagine that you pull the "magnet" away and let the serpent "fall" down back to its opposite end before returning with the magnet replaced. Remember that you are a spiritual being having a human experience, as many have said elsewhere. Your crown chakra holds your purest potential, and shakti energy responds well to that once you reclaim it as your energetic "source."

Change your Mindset

There are a few unintentional roadblocks that tend to come up for many kundalini practitioners. Mainly, you'll want to perform a couple of checks to ensure that your mindset is as aligned with kundalini awakening as possible. Reject as many sources of negativity in your life as you can. If you can't get rid of them, try to face them and call them out, or you could just out-right ignore them. On a personal level, too, you can work to change negativity into its opposite extreme of expression when it comes to your personality traits, your routines, habits, and more. Furthermore, the less attachment you have to material things and patterns, the more open you become to the changes awakening has in store for you. Overall, therefore, reject (and possibly counteract) negativity and attachment, and you will surely flourish. (As a general note, if this method doesn't work for you, don't force yourself to attempt it, especially if it creates toxic effects for you. In that case, you may have a blockage of third eye or crown chakra that needs to be worked through before full awakening can be achieved).

Other Practices That Can Help

In addition to those 29 kundalini-boosters, 6 or so more intensive practices can be added to your daily routine to your benefit. Ranging from physical exercise to dietary change and other modes of subtle energy healing, the methods in this section are gateways to apply to your awakening for strengthening, deepening, and intensifying the experience as it stands. Now it all depends on what you feel comfortable with and what you're willing to draw into your life.

Start Running

One thing you can do is start running if you're physically able to. Running is great for your lungs, your heart, your bones, your posture, and more. Spiritually, running can connect you with the potential you have to free yourself from restriction (to a certain degree) and to create your own reality. When you're in the practice of running, and things really feel good, you have the sense that you are free to go anywhere your feet can carry you. This feeling evokes pure joy for me, and it helps me resolve feelings of being trapped in the system in other ways. For others, too, running can provide those feelings they're desperately craving while increasing their bodies' strengths and potentials. Through the practice of running, you should focus your attention on becoming strong, gaining endurance, and increasing the alignment of your body. If you find that you struggle with any of these three points despite your shift into running, you may want to eliminate it from your routine. The goal here is to promote overall health, and if you're adding undue stress to your days, it's not really worth it in the long run. Instead of running, these individuals are invited to try bicycling, trail walking, road walking, roller blading, or any other, less-intensive method of getting outside and getting physical.

Change your Diet

It can be the case that your diet keeps you from following through with awakening. What vibration do the foods that you're eating contain? Have you ever thought to look? Sure, you've thought of calories, fats, carbs, and proteins, but have you thought of the food's actual vibration? If you're trying to awaken the source of subtle yet universal energy inside you, you're going to need some vibrationally powerful food. If you're running into struggles with awakening that either aren't being resolved or that feel like they're leading nowhere, try switching up your diet. Trade out the processed foods for whole foods. Trade out the meats for fruits and vegetables. Once you start eating better foods and drinking better things, your cells will replenish themselves with the nutrients from these healthier substances, which will lead to a better and healthier overall expression of you! It might sound far-fetched, but food has energy just like crystals and herbs do, even more so. When you eat that food, you take on its energy, and if you eat death constantly, you will have a stagnant vibration. Raise your vibration through your food, and kundalini will be riding those shakti, world-shattering waves to awakening right along with you.

Boost Your Practice with other Subtle Energy-Healing Techniques

While kundalini awakening clearly connects you with realms of subtle energy in your life, it can also be greatly boosted by the presence of other subtle energy-healing modalities aside from just using healing crystals or being around physical nature. Moreover, of course, once you come to know more and more about subtle energy- healing modalities, you can begin to pair them and combine them generally as you see fit. The point is this: as you work through what helps you and what doesn't, you'll realize that your intuition (aka, your connection to your higher self and more) is stronger and more helpful than almost anything else; you will draw to you the healing that you need, even if it just looks like massage or a plant or a teeny pill that dissolves under your tongue. In that case, your practice of kundalini awakening (or any awakening or ascension, generally) should always be boosted by the application of other subtle energetic modalities, as you see fit. A few options are as follows.

First, you could try using flower essences as a modality of subtle energy healing that supports your kundalini awakening. Flower essences work based on the extracted vibration of one type of flower at a time. Basically, you take (or buy the product created by) a few buds of a particular flower and put them in a clear bowl of water. Then, you set the bowl in the sunshine for 12 hours, either at once or over time, as the sun wills. After that point, you remove the flower buds and bottle the water with a drop or two of brandy as a preservative in each bottle. Voila, you've got flower essences! Now, the fun begins. Just as each person, each color, and each crystal has its own vibration, so does each flower. When the essence of the flower is "extracted," to a certain degree, in the flower essence, you can then orally take the remedy (of a few drops of its liquid a few times a day) and work to cure certain ailments that are attached to one's aura or subtle energetic expression. Flower essences can dissolve chakra blockages, too, without you even realizing that's what they're doing. Look up flower essences, for I promise, you'll be fully amazed with the potential.

Second, you could seek out reiki healing in order to remove your chakras' blockages and help the kundalini along. Reiki healing is a traditional Japanese method of energy work that eliminates obstruction and blockage inside the individual (emotionally, spiritually, intellectually, or otherwise) through the applied insight and potential power of the practitioner. While reiki healing is often paired with massage, it doesn't have to be, for it's really just about the potential for the practitioner to dissolve energy blockages within the individual from afar, through the application of the right energetic methods. Reiki healers don't even necessarily have to be next to you to heal you through their methods. By connecting their own kundalini to shakti, to their spirit guides, and to the earth, these individuals can receive guidance that blasts open your chakras from states away, paving the way for the serpent to flow within you. Just be sure you know what you're getting yourself into before your first session!

Third, you could generally receive massages that aid in blockage release. With or without the addition of reiki, massages are still an incredible thing. They feel amazing (especially when performed by someone you trust), but they do more than just make your skin and muscles feel good. Massages can also help you become more aware of any blockages you might have (i.e., through where it feels okay to be touched and where it doesn't, through the places the masseuse tends to linger on, through the pains you didn't realize you had, and more) as you work through that chakra opening and clearing process, making way for kundalini. If you're not comfortable with massage, try just getting a manicure or a pedicure (Even if you're a guy! Just be brave, schedule the appointment, and own it!). The manicurist or pedicurist will absolutely massage your hands or feet, respectively, and that smaller, focused massage will, through reflexology, affect your overall bodily awareness (and potential for kundalini awakening), too. In fact, any reflexology, acupuncture, or acupressure would be equally helpful to this extent.

Fourth, you could still seek out therapy if you're comfortable doing so. While it doesn't help all people, talking things out can still be immensely helpful for some. Therapy doesn't have to be completely about talk, either. Remember from earlier in this chapter that therapy can be based around art, color, sound, and music, too! If you think that you need to work through something in a bigger way than just your insides can handle, don't be ashamed. Turning to therapy may potentially save your life. It might be daunting to know where to start or how to make the first move. Try art or music therapy first if you can. If you can't afford a personal doctor, create your own therapies. Do whatever you need to in order to get the toxicity out and somehow neutralized, and if that means that you go to a "shrink" and talk things over, go for it. Kundalini (and your higher self) will be thankful you did.

Fifth, you could try using essential oils or herbal healing to get things in gear. These suggestions are correlated through their reliance on the vibrational essences of plants and herbs. Through essential oils, the vibration is extracted and contained in oil vehicles, while the herbs could also be made into "flower" essences. Through herbal healing, as a whole, however, herbs are simply appreciated for the subtle energies they contain and the healing they can impart. Essential oils can vary in rarity and availability, but herbs themselves can sometimes be extracted from your own backyard. If you're in a rush these days, however, you can always buy online. Make sure that you're buying essential oils that are perfectly in line with your goals, but you can also make things purposefully ritualistic and low-tech. If you'd rather try the in-person, low-tech method, go out in nature yourself and forage for plants with a guidebook. If you're drawn to a plant without knowing what it is, look it up and take notes. You may find that your guides (or your intuition) have been leading you to the ideal cure for so long without you even knowing it. Whether you use the essential oil, the bought plant, or the foraged herb, kundalini will be grateful and respond in kind.

Sixth, you could try decalcifying your pineal gland and reprogramming your energy through sun gazing. Sun gazing requires you to be present for sunrise and sunset each day. The gist is this: you stand barefoot in the rays of the sun as it rises and sets, looking toward the sun, soaking in its life-giving energy, and learning to feel full of its potential. Then, you tie this practice in with intermittent or spontaneous fasting to get the whole experience of feeling connected to the earth in completely new ways. Sun gazing supposedly has anti- aging, anti-hunger, and anti-illness benefits that are almost unmatched by modern medicine, and you'd better believe that sun gazing will affect kundalini's movement, too. Wake up with the sun and breathe in its rays deeply. If you don't feel kundalini stir up some shakti after just a week, I'll be completely flabbergasted.

Seventh and finally, you could try homeopathic remedies to work through what's causing those chakra blockages within you in the first place. While modern medicine and pharmaceutical cures operate off of allopathic healing (things different from the problem cure the problem) principles, subtle energy cures lead us to investigate the older practice of homeopathy (like cures like) instead. Homeopathy sometimes gets a bad reputation but is much more worth one's effort than you might imagine. Homeopathic remedies are constructed from the vibrational essences of plants, minerals, and animals to the point of mitigating the debilitating circumstances or illnesses. Instead of assuming, like modern medicine does, that you can only heal something by administering a cure devised separately, homeopathy assumes that poisons (in very small doses) can actually heal greater ailments. It's worth writing a whole book on the subject, but for now, it will suffice to say that you should look into homeopathy if you're intrigued by this point. It could be that the trigger for your kundalini awakening is a teeny homeopathy pill you'll let dissolve under your tongue, and the greatest thing is that if you take a homeopathic cure that your body doesn't actually need, it won't do anything to you at all. Essentially, these wonderful subtle energetic remedies only work if you need them. What are you waiting for? You'll never know how well these remedies can work until you do the research and try them for yourself!

Chapter 9: The Poses

Now for the part we've all been waiting for: the asanas (poses)! As I mentioned earlier on in the book, please remember that you should go at your own pace. If you feel like 10 minutes is enough for you each day that's wonderful and you'll get a solid base level introduction to practicing yoga. However, if you prefer to spend more time on each pose I highly recommend it.

As you get more comfortable do each pose that you've learned up until the day you are on. For instance, if you're on Day 5: do all poses 1-4 up until Day 5 so that they stay fresh in your memory and you can build on the flexibility you're developing with each pose.

Ready? Let's get started.

Day 1: Mountain Pose

This pose might look like you're just standing there, but if done correctly it serves a much greater purpose and is generally the starting position for other standing poses.

Step 1: Stand upright so that your big toes are completely flat and touching the floor. Keep your feet about hip width apart and parallel to one another. Now, flex your toes upward and wide—really stretch. This is going to gauge whether or not you're balancing your posture correctly. If you lose balance then most likely you're not centering your weight evenly on all points of your feet so you need to correct your balance so that it's spread evenly on your feet.

Step 2: Contract your thigh muscles and try to lift your kneecaps, but do so without contracting your lower abdomen. Lift the inside of your ankles to help strengthen those inner arches and visualize an imaginary line of energy that spreads the length of your inner thighs to your groin and then from your core (or torso) to your neck, head— all the way out exiting through the crown of your head. Now turn your upper thighs slightly inward and visualize lengthening the tailbone down to the floor while lifting your pubic bone toward your belly button.

Step 3: Now focus on pressing your shoulder blades back and then slowly stretch them out and release down your back. Lift the upper part of your sternum toward the ceiling without pushing the lower part of your ribs outward. Widen and stretch the collarbones, then hang your arms at your sides, palms facing forward.

Step 4: Finally, balance your head completely above the center of your pelvic area. Make sure that your chin is parallel to the floor and keep your mouth and throat soft as well as your eyes.

Stay here and breathe slowly and intentionally for 1 minute or however long you feel comfortable.

Day 2: Tree Pose

Step 1: First, stand in Mountain pose and begin to shift your weight a little bit onto your left foot. Keep the inside of the foot firm on the floor and bend the right knee. Slowly reach down and grab your right ankle with your right hand.

Step 2: Pull your right foot up and place it against your inner left thigh as high as you can to where it feels comfortable. Your goal should eventually be to press your right heel into your left groin completely flat with your toes pressing down toward the floor. Keep your pelvic bone directly over your left foot.

Step 3: Visualize lengthening your tailbone, getting it as long as you can. Press your right foot into your inner thigh and then place your hands in the prayer position in front of you, looking straight ahead.

If you don't want to put your hands in prayer position you can place them on your hips or at your sides.

Stay in this position for 1 minute, breathing evenly. After you've completed this, go back to Mountain pose and do Tree pose with your opposite leg.

Day 3: Bridge Pose

Step 1: Begin by lying flat on your back. Bring your knees up to a 90- degree angle and placc your fcct flat on the floor with your heels as close to your glutes as possible.

Step 2: Exhale while pressing your feet and arms firmly into the floor, contract your tailbone up toward your pubic bone and firm your buttocks muscles. Now lift your butt off the floor keeping everything parallel.

Step 3: Place your hands below your back on the floor either flat or you can clasp them together if that's more comfortable. Keep your abdomen muscles engaged and try to lengthen your back.

Step 4: Keep your chin lifted slightly above your sternum and your shoulder blades firm. To keep your shoulders from closing in, firm your outer arms and broaden the shoulder blades, stretching them across the base of your neck. Stay in this pose for 1 minute and when you're ready to come out of it, do so by exhaling and rolling each of your vertebrae slowly down onto the floor.

Day 4: Extended Triangle Pose

Step 1: Stand in Mountain pose and as you exhale, spread your legs about 3-4 feet apart. Place your arms in the air parallel to the floor and then reach out to your sides, shoulders wide, palms facing down.

Step 2: Position your left foot slightly to the right and then place your right foot at 90 degrees. Rotate your right thigh so that it's facing outward and the center of your right knee is in line with your ankle.

Step 3: Now, exhale and bend your torso to the right placing it over your right leg. Do not bend at the waist, but rather at your hip. Strengthen your left leg and press your left heel into the floor. Rotate your torso to the left and let your left hip move forward a bit.

Step 4: Next you can rest your right hand however is comfortable— on the floor, your ankle, shin, etc. Now, stretch and raise your left arm up high to the ceiling lining it up with your shoulders. Be sure to keep your head neutral or you can turn to the left to look up at your left thumb.

Stay in this pose for 1 minute and then slowly inhale and come out of it by raising your arm toward the ceiling and pressing your back heel into the floor. Follow the same steps for your opposite side.

Day 5: Half Twist

Step 1: Sit on the floor with your legs flat in front of you. Bend your left knee and place your left leg over your right so that your left foot is resting on the floor at the edge of your right hip.

Step 2: Now, move your right foot over your left knee so that it's positioned outside of the thigh. Be sure to keep both sides of your butt evenly on the ground.

Step 3: Next you're going to lean back onto your right hand and then inhale while place your left arm over your head to lengthen your torso and spine.

Step 4: As you exhale twist to your right and bring your left elbow outside of the right thigh. Look over your right shoulder and be sure to keep length in your neck. As you continue to inhale try to lengthen your spine more. As you exhale, twist deeper into the pose.

Stay in this position, inhaling and exhaling for 1 minute. As you come out of the pose, do it on the exhale and release gently. Switch to the opposite side.

Day 6: Cat-Cow

Step 1: Start with both hands and knees on the floor. Be sure to keep your knees under the hips and wrists under the shoulders. Your spine should be neutral and back flat. Keep your abdominal muscles engaged and breath in deeply.

Step 2: As you exhale, round the spine upward as far as you can towards the ceiling. It helps if you imagine pulling your belly button into your spine. At the same time pull your chin into your chest and relax your neck. This would be considered the cat pose.

Step 3: When you inhale, arch the back and relax your stomach, keeping everything loose. Raise your head and tailbone upward making sure not to add pressure to your neck. This would be considered the cow pose.

Step 4: Flow back and forth from cat to cow for as long as you like, just be sure to connect the movements with your breathing and really stay conscious of each vertebrae as you inhale and exhale.

Again, you can do this for as long as you wish. It's a great spinal warming exercise and helps alleviate low back pain. I recommend at least 1 minute.

Day 7: Legs-Up-The-Wall Pose

Step 1: Determine the distance you need to be from the wall: if you're tall move farther away, if you're shorter get closer and adjust as needed. If you feel like this pose puts too much pressure on your lower back or you're uncomfortable, you can use a rolled up towel or a bolster to provide support in your lower back.

Step 2: Sit sideways and start with your right side facing the wall, as you exhale, swiftly bring your legs up onto the wall in one fluid movement and then slowly lower your shoulders and head onto the floor. If you feel like you need support at the base of your neck feel free to place a rolled up towel or wash cloth there to ease the pressure.

Step 3: Be mindful of the position of your chin—make sure you're not pushing it into your chest. Keep your shoulders pressed down flat towards the floor and place your arms out at your sides, palms facing upward.

Step 4: Keep the legs slightly taut to keep them from "drooping" and then sink the weight of your lower body down toward your pelvic floor.

Stay in this pose for as long as you like—it's exceptionally comfortable for getting into a meditative state. Just be sure that when you come out of the pose you're not twisting your back, but rather roll gently to one side instead.

Day 8: Cobra Pose

Step 1: Lie on your stomach in the floor with your legs out behind you and the tops of your feet touching the floor. Next, place your hands on the floor directly under your shoulders as you press your elbows back and into your sides.

Step 2: Place pressure on the tops of your feet and thighs and pubic bone as you press yourself firmly into the floor. As you inhale, straighten your arms and lift your chest off the floor. Make sure that you don't go so far that you're pubic bone is off the floor.

Step 3: Keep your shoulder blades firm as you "puff" your chest forward, lifting through the top of your sternum. Be mindful not to tighten your lower back. If you notice quite a bit of lower back pain or pressure, feel free to widen the distance between your legs as this should help.

Stay in this pose for 30 seconds as you continue to breathe slowly and evenly. On the exhale you can release.

Day 9: Standing Forward Bend

Step 1: Stand in Mountain pose with your hands on your hips. As you exhale, bend slowly forward at your hips. At the same time you should be drawing your stomach inward and engaging your abdominal muscles. You want to focus on lengthening your mid- section as you descend.

Step 2: Now, with your knees as straight as you can keep them, place your fingertips or palms on the floor in front of you. If this is too much of a stretch just grab wherever you can reach to—maybe your ankles or even your calves. Remember not to push yourself too hard.

Step 3: Press your heels into the floor and lift your butt into the air. As you inhale, focus on lengthening your mid-section. As you exhale release yourself deeper into the forward bend.

Step 4: Be mindful of your neck and keep it loose—let it hang freely.

Stay in this pose for 1 minute and then gently bring yourself out of it by unrolling your torso as you inhale.

Day 10: Extended Side Angle

This pose is somewhat similar to the Extended Triangle—the difference being that instead of both legs staying straight you will come down into a lunge position with the leg you're leaning into.

Step 1: Stand in Mountain pose and as you exhale, spread your legs about 3-4 feet apart. Place your arms in the air parallel to the floor and then reach out to your sides, shoulders wide, palms facing down.

Step 2: Rotate your right thigh outward and keep your kneecap in line with your right ankle. Now, you're going to roll your left hip forward and to the right, but make sure you're upper torso goes back and to the left.

Step 3: Firmly keep your left heel planted into the floor and as you exhale bend your right knee into a lunge position over your right ankle, making sure not to go past your toes. Try to aim for your right thigh being parallel to the floor.

Step 4: Keep your shoulder blades firm and extend your left arm up to the ceiling, turning your palm to face your head. As you inhale, reach your left arm over your left ear. Focus on stretching and lengthening your entire left side of your body. As you do so, look up at your left arm and also be mindful to lengthen your right side of your torso as well.

Step 5: As you exhale press the right side of your mid-section down onto your right thigh and press the fingertips of your right hand onto the floor. Your right thigh should be parallel with the floor.

Stay here and breathe for 1 minute, focusing on staying as open as possible. Reverse your feet and do the same thing for your left side.

Day 11: Camel Pose

Step 1: Get on the floor with your knees hip width apart. Visualize yourself drawing your glutes up into your body, but keep your hips soft while you plant your shins and tops of the feet into the floor.

Step 2: Place your hands on your hips as you rest your palms on your butt with your fingers pointing down. As you inhale, keep your shoulder blades pressed back and your head high. Ideally you want to keep your thighs perpendicular to the floor, but if you're a beginner it's perfectly okay to give yourself some slack. If you can't go straight back to touch your feet you can turn slightly to one side and place your hand on your foot, then go back to the neutral position and place your other hand on your other foot.

Step 3: Make sure to lift your pelvic bone upward and focus on lengthening your spine and releasing pressure. As you do so place your hands against your heels and your fingers pointing down to your toes. Don't squeeze your shoulder blades together and don't tighten your neck or throat area.

Stay in this pose for up to 1 minute, however long is comfortable to you. If you feel pressure in your lower back you can counteract this pose by going into Child's pose for a minute or so.

Chapter 10: Chakra Healing

Easy and Natural Ways to Heal Your Chakras

Now that you know the main chakras, it is time to learn how you can heal your chakras. Healing your chakras is important to ensure good physical health. If your chakras have blockages or are not functioning properly, then the physical body will also become ill. Studies show that before any ailment manifests in the physical plane, it first manifests in the spiritual realm. Of course, the health of your chakras does not just pertain to your physical health, but also to the qualities and attributes of the chakras concerned.

So, how do you heal chakras easily and naturally? Remember that the chakras are connected to your physical body. By maintaining a healthy body, you also get to empower the chakras. Therefore, to keep your chakras healthy, you should keep your body healthy. The problem comes when you consider how to maintain a healthy physical body. Many people say that you should eat chicken and poultry products to gain protein and other "healthy" nutrients. However, as far as spirituality is concerned, especially if you want to awaken your Kundalini, it is advised that you stay away from eating meat and poultry products. Instead, you should observe a vegan or vegetarian diet. It is also worth noting that there are studies that have proven that eating meat can cause lots of diseases, including diabetes and cancer, among others. If you find it hard to stay away from meat and poultry, then at least try to minimize your consumption of the said products.

Doing regular exercise is also encouraged. In fact, exercising is one of the body's natural ways to remove negative energies from your system. You do not need to engage in a heavy workout. A light workout like walking or jogging would be enough. Simply put, everything that is good for the physical body is also good for your chakras. Indeed, this is another reason for you to be healthy.

Heal Your Chakras Through Meditation

The best way to work on your chakras is through meditation. Of course, this does not mean that adopting a healthy lifestyle is no longer important. Remember that when you treat or heal something, you also need to look into the main cause or source of the problem. Hence, if you know that it is your lifestyle that is continuously bringing you unhealthy and dirty energies, then you need to make some adjustments.

However, there are certain meditations that work directly to achieve a specific objective. As you go through this book, you will learn different meditation that techniques that not only enhance your overall system and chakras but also specialize in certain parts of your spiritual or energy body. For now, here is an excellent meditation that can help you cleanse and heal your chakras:

Assume a meditative position and relax. Visualize a powerful ray of light descending from heaven and moving down into your crown chakra, charging it with immense power. See and feel your crown chakra being cleansed and recharged. Do not stop until you see and feel that your crown chakra is fully cleansed and is radiating with powerful light. Now, send this divine energy down to the ajna or third eye chakra. Allow the powerful ray of divine light to cleanse and charge your ajna chakra. Once you are satisfied, send the energy to the next chakra, which is the throat chakra. Allow this divine energy to cleanse and supercharge your throat chakra. Next, let the ray of light descend down to your heart chakra. See and feel as your heart chakra shines brilliantly, free from all dirt and negativity. Now, allow the ray for light to descend down to your solar plexus chakra. Allow the light to cleanse and charge this chakra. Send the light further down to your sacral chakra, and feel how the light empowers this chakra. Finally, send the divine light down to your root chakra. Feel yourself being more stable and grounded. Allow this ray of light to fully cleansed and charge your root chakra. Once you have charged and cleansed all your chakras, see and feel all the seven main chakras radiating powerfully and full of brilliance. Visualize the divine ray of light slowly fade away. Say a short prayer and thank God or the universe for cleansing and healing you. Enjoy this moment of divine bliss and peace.

When you are ready to return to ordinary consciousness, gently move your fingers and toes, and slowly open your eyes.

The meditation technique above is one of the best ways to empower and heal the chakras through meditation. You are free to make adjustments or modifications if you want. The important thing is to charge and purify your chakras. The said ray of light can be visualized in any way you want. You can see it having the same color as the chakra being cleansed and charged, but you can also just use white light to make the visualization simpler. After all, the color white is the color of akasha. As such, it possesses all the colors.

It is important to ensure that your chakras are cleansed and energized. This will not just give you good health, but it is also important in awakening the Kundalini, as well as for the development of psychic powers. You can also sensitize your hands and scan your chakras to see if there are chakras that may need healing. It is advised that you cleanse your chakras at least once every week. It is also recommended that you cleanse and energize your chakras after you have been exposed to negative energies.

Chapter 11: Reaching the Higher Self

There are some traditions that divide humans into three selves: the younger, the middle, and the higher. Your younger-self is the subconscious mind. Your middle-self is your regular consciousness. Your higher-self is your god-self. The higher-self tends to be the trickiest for people to understand.

Some traditions view the higher-self as the best version that a person can be. Regardless of how you view the higher-self, the truth is that it is your god-self. The question to answer now is how you can connect with this god-self and how it can benefit you. The answer to this is simpler than you may believe. You can do this through meditation. During meditation, your mind becomes still. After you have cut off your inner chatter, it will create a path to realization and a connection with your higher-self.

This is the way that monks and gurus find their answers. They sit in meditation and allow their minds to become empty. In the end, you will come to the realization that you just know. This is how your higher-self works. Your higher-self always has a connection with the Divine and knows everything.

The younger-self is interested in elaborate rituals and things, while the higher-self wants to find serenity and silence. The more that you are able to quiet your mind, the more you will be able to manifest your higher-self. This is why meditation is one of the most important things you can learn how to do. You don't have to have an intention. All you have to do is allow things to unfold as they will. You will learn how to let things be.

Gaining Clarity

Meditation will allow you to naturally gain clarity and wisdom from your higher or divine self. You can follow any meditation practice that you want to as long as you keep up a regular practice. However, there are some meditation techniques that are designed with this in mind and used for the purpose of connecting with your higher-self. The meditation that we are going to go over is a great meditation for gaining more wisdom and mental clarity so that you can communicate with your higher-self.

1. Get into a relaxed and meditative position. Take a few deep breaths and allow yourself to relax.

2. Once you are relaxed, try to picture yourself as the best version of you. Try not to look at this on a physical level, but on every level, including spiritual, emotional, and mental.

3. Picture this version of yourself standing right in front of you, as if they are getting ready to talk with you. Remember that the person standing in front of you is a highly evolved person and can easily communicate with you through telepathy, so make sure that you pay attention to any thoughts that may come to your mind.

4. Do your best not to try and force thoughts to come to mind. Allow thoughts to come in freely and without any pressure.

5. Turn your focus to your higher-self. Begin to communicate with your higher self in your mind. You don't have to speak out loud. All you have to do is think about the things that you want to say. Keep your mind open to whatever your higher-self tells you. Enjoy this conversation and make sure that you learn from it.

6. Once you have finished your conversation with your higher-self, take a moment to realize that this being you adore for all of its wisdom and brilliance is really a part of you. You are indeed fantastic. All you have to do is recognize the beauty that you naturally have.

7. On your next inhale, feel and watch as you breathe this higher-self back inside of you. While this happens, notice

that everything that you love about your higher-self has now become a part of who you truly are. You are now your higher-self.

8. Take a few more deep breaths as you feel the brilliance and wisdom of your higher-self inside of you. Appreciate this newfound power. You are a beautiful and wonderful person.

When you do this meditation, you can make any adjustments that you feel are necessary to help it work for you. This is a great meditation to use when you want to connect with your higher self and to help you realize the amazing power that lives within you.

Chapter 12: Concentration and Breath for Chakra Healing

Going forward from the last chapter, when you are working on healing your chakras, it is an invaluable tool to have a good grasp on breathing techniques and exercises, as well as powerful concentration. Both of these concepts are the basis of meditation, and this chapter will open you up to understanding what that means and why concentration and breath are imperative for the chakra healing process.

Your energy will always need a place to go and relax and when you can stop, focus on your feelings, and breathe, then you are able to connect with your energy centers in a way that will essentially block unwanted energies from causing a disruption in your balance, as well as helping your return to your center.

The world is full of upheaval and things out of our control, and these types of things are what throw us off course when we are finally just feeling aligned again. Breath and concentration will act as a shield from these outside forces so that you are regularly calling upon your own strength to fight for your own energy more.

You may have already learned a variety of yoga breathing techniques or tips for concentration and focus, and you should always continue finding new and exciting practices that work well for you. In this chapter, we will use a very simple, step-by-step activity to help you understand the power of breath and focus on your chakra system.

If you are new to meditation, then this will be a perfect entry point for you. If you are already practicing meditation techniques, then you are welcome to skip over this section.

Meditation for Breath and Concentration to Heal the Chakras

1) Find a space where you will be undisturbed. Silence your cellphone and put a do not disturb on your door, if desired (you can play meditation music if you prefer to start with some music to help you relax).
2) Find a comfortable seated position. You can sit on the floor with your legs crossed or on a cushion, and you can also use a chair if it is more comfortable.
3) Sit and take a few moments to adjust until you feel fully comfortable.
4) Make sure your spine is straight. If you are in a chair, be sure to keep your feet flat on the floor.
5) Place your hands comfortably on your knees, palms up.
6) Take an inhale in through your nostrils for a count of 5 seconds.
7) Hold the breath for 5 seconds.
8) Exhale for 5 seconds.
9) Repeat. In for 5, hold for 5, out for 5. Repeat this step 5 times.
10) After you have finished this round of breaths, concentrate your attention on your body starting at your feet. Begin scanning your feet, ankles, and toes for any tension.
11) When you find some tension in this part of you, take a deep breath in for 5 seconds and as you hold the breath for 5 seconds, picture the tension preparing to release from your body. As you exhale for 5 seconds, release the tension from your feet, toes, and ankles.
12) Move up to your legs (knees, shins, thighs, etc.) and scan for any tension. Perform the same action on the legs that you did in the previous step. Breath in for 5, collect the tension as you hold for 5, release the tension for 5 on the exhale.
13) Continue this activity through your whole body and use your chakras as markers of where to concentrate on releasing the tension. When you have made it to the top of the head at the

crown chakra, and you have completed the tension release in all of the chakras, end the tension scanning in the shoulders, arms, and hands.

14) Breathe in for 5, collect the arm, hand, and shoulder tension while you hold for 5, and then exhale for 5.
15) Now that you have released the tension from your body, you can practice deeper breath within each chakra. The next series of steps will be repeated for each chakra, starting at the root and going up to the crown.
16) Take a long breath in for a count of ten. Hold the breath for ten. Then, release the breath in an exhale for ten.
17) Focusing on the root chakra, picture it in your mind as you take in the next breath for a ten count. See its color, light, shape, and size inside of your body.
18) Hold the inhale for a count of ten, and while you do, see the root chakra preparing to grow in size and clarity. See it getting ready to release any tension.
19) As you exhale for a count of ten, see your root chakra enlarge slightly as it pushes out any tension and unwanted energies.
20) Repeat steps 16-19 with the root chakra at least three times before moving up the spine to the sacral chakra.
21) Once you are ready to move to the sacral chakra, you can perform the same actions you did with the root chakra (steps 16-20).
22) You will continue these steps through every chakra, steps 16- 20, moving up one more chakra after you finish your breath and concentration meditation for the one before. For the most effective results, perform steps 16-19 for each chakra at least 3 times or more.
23) Return your focus to your whole body once you have finished your breath and concentration meditations. Spend a few moments taking several inhales for 5, and release for 5. In for 5, out for 5.
24) When you are ready, you can return to your daily activities.
25) Using a breathing and concentration meditation like this one is a powerful tool to help you reorganize your energy and help you maintain all of the possible levels of basic chakra

methods for awakening, healing, balancing, strengthening. It is simple, effective, and easy and won't take up a lot of time.

26) You can modify this practice and incorporate other, more yogic styles of breathing if you are familiar with some of those methods. Anything you do to bring additional breath and focus to the experience will be beneficial to you.
27) In the next chapter, you will learn the basics of how crystal, oils, and herbs are effective in treating the symptoms of a blocked chakra system.

Chapter 13: Kundalini Exercises

Just as with the yoga and meditation kundalini exercises, we must be confident that we are prepared for these practices. Approach these advanced exercises just as you have been with your routine, find your practice space, clear your mind, have an empty stomach, and overall be respectful of kundalini.

We have spent the duration of this book preparing you for this moment. We are now stepping through the threshold of beginner to adept. When we first begin these practices, we see dramatic change take place early on our path. The more adapted to become to this energetic lifestyle, the more it becomes a normal aspect of your life. This may make it more difficult to see the changes taking place, or perhaps you've found a balanced and livable practice. Either way, as you progress, you will notice that the kundalini energy is much different than working with the chakras or moving your body's energy around as practice. The kundalini energy will be more intense and will engulf these other energies as its own, optimizing the healing qualities and taking you to the next level of these ancient practices.

Kundalini should be approached with the utmost respect. You may even wish to leave an offering or prayer before your practice advances. As we begin these practices let's keep in mind the power of the present moment. Just as a meditation practice aims to achieve, our mind is clearest in the present moment. We are the most attentive and efficient when we are at this moment. We need to maintain this focus when working with kundalini. She requires our attention and respect as we wake her. We do not want to startle her or anger her as we approach these techniques. We must be in the most attentive and focused state that we have ever experienced to achieve the results we seek,

One final note before the exercises begin: Listen to your body. If you do not feel that you are ready to approach kundalini, then absolutely do not do it! There is no shame in being honest with yourself about your practice. Like we have mentioned throughout this book, not everyone will progress in the same way as everyone else. We need to be honest with ourselves about our progress and be truthful when we ask ourselves if we are ready. For what it's worth, the more practice you have before approaching the serpent, the more likely you will be successful in your endeavors. Take your time and be patient. Hone your skills and have an enjoyable experience as you do. This is not a career or a job. There is no deadline or strict structure. Create your own personal path by listening to your body and mind. You will intuitively know that you are ready when you are ready, do not approach kundalini until you are sure that you will be able to adhere to your promises to her.

Starting Out

As we mentioned, the present moment is key to these practices. Stay in this moment and do not worry about the past or future. If you can to stay in the present moment, you will begin to dissolve the deepest illusions your mind has been constantly creating about the true reality of nature. You can start by seeing the reality of the endless energy of divine bliss in everyone and everything. This bliss is always there. We just need to see it. If we buy into the delusions of the chaotic mind at any moment, our kundalini working will have failed, and we will need to start over. This is very common, so do not be discouraged.

By staying consciously here in this eternal moment, the phenomena of psychic abilities, unseen powers, and magical manifestation will naturally begin to happen in your life. Combined with the practices in this book, we can optimize these powers. Kundalini will give you the capacity to attract anything in the world you desire. Since these practices act to merge the kundalini's infinite power with your subtle energetic and physical bodies, we are effectively upgrading our existence. This upgrade may even protect us from emotional attacks or various otherworldly disasters.

As we are willing to live in this present moment, we will empower ourselves as individuals. With these kundalini workings, we can essentially tap into the source of the universe and keep it near throughout our lives. Sure, we can work with our chakras with kundalini still dormant, but to get the absolute most out of these practices we will need kundalini to be awake, piercing our chakras and opening them fully to the universal power. When each of the seven chakra centers in your body is ignited, you will transverse the world as you know it. No longer bound to time or worry. The God and Goddess, Shiva and Shakti, within you will become very apparent, and you will know without a doubt, that powers that are inherent in your body and mind. From this point, there is no turning back, your life is altered completely, and you now are familiar with some secrets of the universe.

Practices

The following practices will combine what we have learned throughout this book. Meditation, yoga, mantra and visualization is the key component of the following exercises. These practices are the most complex and challenging and are specifically designed for kundalini awakening.

Keep the serpent energy in mind as you practice these exercises. Visualize the dormant snake at the base of your spine, imagine the infinite potential in the awakening of this energy that is a fiery spark of consciousness just waiting to rise inside of you. As you take on these final practices, you will awake this energy. If you have put in the time and effort, you will build this relationship with kundalini. This energy may rise slowly, or gradually make itself known, but there are many times that this energy bursts out of its slumber, rise aggressively through your spine. Many have described this feeling online and in spiritual communities. This flood of life is incredible and changes the lives of the experiencers forever. Raising this energy will essentially begin your new life, you will be living fully for the first time. There is an infinite potential of where to go from that point, eventually unifying Shakti and Shiva, allowing them to dance the creative expression of oneness through you.

Kundalini Exercise 1

This is a sequence of exercises that ignites the fire within in hopes of waking kundalini. The mantras used is related to the name of truth and acts to stimulate our entire being with its vibration. The yoga poses and visualization act to engage your energetic body as well as your physical body to really get the energy moving.

Practice these exercises after your body is sufficiently warmed up after some light yoga or breathing exercises.

1. Kneel onto your knees, sitting on the heels of your feet.

2. Inhale and bend forward touching your brow to the ground

3. Breathe deeply for ten breaths, relaxing into the position.

4. Chant the following mantra, internally or out loud: Sat, Sat, Sat, Sat, Sat, Sat, Naam.

As you chant, each Sat should be vibrated into a chakra, starting with the root and rising through the other chakras until we reach the crown chakra and chant Naam. Continue this exercise for ten minutes, then move onto the next step for Kundalini exercise 1.

After you have completed, the Sat Naam exercise, you can begin the next sequence. This practice is simple and helps to relax after the Sat Naam practice.

5. Raise your brow from the floor.

6. Slowly stretch your legs outward, extending them in front of you.

7. Straighten your back and raise your hands above your head.

8. Bend at the hips and try to grab your toes, hold this position.

9. Breathe deeply for seven breaths.

Each of the seven breaths should engage a chakra. Visualize the breath penetrating the root chakra, then upward through the other chakras until your seventh breath. After the seventh breath, immediately move onto the next sequence.

This part of the exercise is a winding down of sorts. You will feel the energy in your body shift dramatically. Take note of the changes you experience as you relax.

10. Raise up from touching your toes then lay down on your back.

11. Relax your body with your hands at your sides. Breathe deeply.

12. Lay here motionless for seven minutes.

As you lay quietly, visualize kundalini lying dormant. Not unlike your motionless body, she lays asleep. Visualize her as a literal snake, just let the details come as they will.

Once you have reached seven minutes, rise up slowly, visualizing kundalini awakening. Sit quietly with your visualization and see what happens. Sit quietly and breathe normally.

This is the end of the first kundalini exercise, but after you relaxed, you can perform it again and again. It is best not to perform this exercise more than three times per day.

Kundalini Exercise 2

This sequence of exercises is designed for purification of the body and chakras. It acts as an overall clearing and opening, making way for the kundalini energy to rise. This purification is much needed in a world of synthetic drugs and foods. This exercise pairs well after long work weeks or before healing baths.

1. Stand up straight, balancing your weight on our feet.
2. Stretch your leg behind you with the top of your foot staying on the ground.

3. Bend the other leg until you have a ninety-degree angle at your knee, your weight will be on the bent leg.
4. Place your palms together, and hold at your chest, focus your vision on your brow.
5. Deep breathe in this position.
6. Stand up and switch legs performing the same exercise. This practice is a physical work out that helps to get the body moving and engage the chakras in preparation for the next sequence.

7. Sit down and cross your legs comfortably.
8. Put your hands on your hips and raise your diaphragm.
9. Breathe deeply in this position for three minutes.

The next sequence is more intensive, you can view the first sequences as a warm-up for the next ones.

10. Stay seated and breathing consistently.

11. Interlock your hands at your chest, forearms parallel to the floor.

12. Inhale as deep as you can.

13. Forcibly exhale all the breath as fast as you can.

14. Inhale fully and hold breath.

15. Exhale completely and forcibly.

16. Continue this practice for three minutes.

We should be raising the energy up through the chakras as we practice this, the forced breaths engaging the solar plexus chakra and heart chakra. The next sequence contacts the throat and third eye chakras.

17. Stay seated with your legs crossed.

18. Extend the arms out at the sides like wings.

19. Roll your eyes up gazing at your brow.

20. Breathe deeply and hold this position for 3 minutes.

21. Press your hands together and straighten your spine.

22. Push firm on your hands and hold this position for three minutes.

This exercise is excellent for purification purposes but also works directly with kundalini energy. Visualizing kundalini being purified with this practice can add to the potency as well.

Exercise for Blockages

This exercise is great for clearing blockages in your chakras and nadis. It acts as a great precursor to kundalini works, while also engaging the kundalini. Practice this exercise on a weekly basis. It ensures your chakras do not become clogged.

1. Sit with your legs crossed and raise your hands over your head. Practice a range of motion stretching your arms in circles.
2. Clinch your fists at your heart and roll your shoulders forward and backward.

This exercise becomes quite fun as you move through the steps quickly. It can almost become a dance of sorts. This exercise can be performed before an intensive yoga or meditation session to get the energy flowing smoothly.

A Note on Ancestral Lineage

This exercise is great for breaking ancestral blockages as well. Consider all the people in your ancestral line, only a small fraction of them that you have actually met. These lines can get blocked just as energetic channels get blocked by day to day life. There may be criminals or other troublemakers in this lineage.

The advanced techniques of working to clear our energetic ancestral lineage are powerful and complex. Use the blockage exercises above to heal your ancestral lines visually. You can imagine the line of ancestors going all the way back to the source of consciousness, healing it along the way. You may even want to leave offerings or call upon your ancestors to assist you in this work.

Ancestral practices are very complex and would need a whole book to explore properly. For now, use the blockage techniques to clear your family line.

Chakra Balancing Exercise

Stimulating the chakra system at least once per day is good practice to ensure that your chakras will not become blocked or unbalanced in the future. Deep breathing exercises and a consistent yoga routine go a long way to achieve this balanced system, but we also must practice more intensive exercises as well, especially if we have yet to awaken the kundalini energy.

1. In a standing position, place your feet shoulder-width apart.
2. Squat down so the thighs are parallel to the floor.
3. Reach towards your toes, placing the palms on top of the feet be sure to keep your back straight.
4. Lift your head and look forward.
5. Move to kneeling position, sit on the heels, and stretch the arms straight over your head.
6. Interlock your fingers except for the index fingers, which should be pointing straight up.
7. Begin to chant 'Sat Naam' emphatically in a constant rhythm.
8. On Naam relax the stomach.
9. Continue for three minutes.

This exercise is great for stimulating the entire chakra system. The second section continues this practice. If you wish to practice the above before moving on to the second sequence, then do so until you are fully prepared to perform the entire exercise. This is your practice, so make it what you want and go at your own pace.

11. Kneel sitting on your heels, rest the hands on the thighs.

12. Begin inhaling in short sips through your pursed lips until the lungs are full of air.

13. With your breath held, raise up and rotate the hips around in a circle.

14. Exhale and sit back down on your heels.

15. Move to a lying position and bring the hands to the Navel Point. The left hand is closest to the body, and the right hand is over the left.

This is a great exercise for learning to feel the chakras as well. Step 16 is essentially asking you to use your hands in circular motions to feel and manipulate the chakras. Move on with the next steps after you have sufficiently felt and moved the chakras.

17. Remain on your back and extend your arms straight above you.

18. Make fists of your hands and pull your fists into your chest.

19. Release your clenched fists and repeat three more times.

20. Resting on your back, place the left hand on the heart and the right hand over the left.

21. Breathe deeply and engage your heart chakra.

22. Release your fists and place your hands at your sides

23. Lay comfortably for five to ten minutes.

This exercise acts to clear away chakra blockages while also acting as a great warm-up exercise to start your day or begin your kundalini practices. These complex exercises have so many steps because this is the amount of effort needed to stimulate the kundalini energy.

The kundalini exercises above are the methods that will skyrocket your practice from a humble beginner's practice to a full-fledged advanced routine. When these exercises are practiced consistently and approached with respect and seriousness, you will surely open your chakras and awaken the kundalini energy. These practices should all be performed on an empty stomach to avoid cramps or indigestion. This is why we recommend performing them in the morning when you first awake. Your belly will be empty, and you will have a fresh canvas to work with as you start your day. Not to mention these exercises really get the blood moving, you may even be able to skip your coffee!

Chapter 14: 5-Minute Meditation Sessions

The following meditation can be applied for about 5 minutes, but you are also free to use them for as long as you would like. These are excellent meditation techniques for beginners, and they can have profound effects. The more you practice these meditation techniques, the better you will get.

- ✓ **Affirmation Meditation**

You are probably aware of the use of affirmations. For example, when people are feeling afraid, you might hear them say, "I can do this." It is like affirming what they want to happen. Although this is something that is very common, the truth is that only a few know how to use it properly. What you need to know is that affirmations are more effective when they are recited in a meditative state. But, before we discuss them meditation technique itself, you should know how to create your own affirmation. Here are the steps:

Keep it short and clear

You should keep your affirmation short and to the point. As a rule, try to make it just a short and single sentence only. Take note that you will be reciting, almost like chanting, your affirmation, so do not make it too long. Just around less than 10 words would be nice. Also, avoid using hard to understand words. Instead, use simple words that are easy to understand. Examples: I am strong, I am courageous, I am feeling better every day, I am happy, I am healthy, I am getting stronger, and the likes.

Use the present tense

When you make an affirmation, you should use the present tense. Do not say, "I will become a clairvoyant." Instead, you should say, "I am a clairvoyant." Consider this as some kind of trick of the mind, if you would. The reason here is that if you use the future tense, then it might happen only after so many years; and if you use the past tense, then it means that it no longer needs to happen. Therefore, you should use the present tense, to make it manifest right now or at least as soon as possible.

Believe

It is also important that you believe in what you affirm. Without faith, then it would not be of any good. But, as the saying goes, "With faith, nothing is impossible." Therefore, believe in what you affirm. Believe that it has been realized already, and it shall come true. Again, consider this some form of a trick of the mind, but this is how the universal law works and is the secret to make your desires turn into reality. If you do not believe in what you say, then the affirmation loses its power.

Repeat

While you are in a meditative state, you should repetition your affirmation as many times as you may need to make it sink into your subconscious. Use it as a kind of mantra or focus of your meditation. Let your mind absorb it and sink into its meaning. Let your affirmation be the sound of the universe at that moment.

Only use one affirmation

It is not good to use different kinds of affirmations at once. Just focus on one affirmation, and do not change it until you have achieved its objective or if you are ready to just give it up. Using more than one affirmation at the same time can be confusing, and your mind might now know which affirmation to absorb fully. Hence, do it one at a time.

Now that you know the important points about making an affirmation, it is time to move on to the actual meditation process:

Assume a meditative posture and relax. Be sure that you already have an affirmation that you want to use. Do any basic meditation, such as the breathing meditation. The objective is simply to reach a meditative state. Once you reach a trance or meditative state, start saying your affirmation. Use your affirmation as the point of focus of your meditation. Focus on it and be one with it.

When you are ready to end this meditation, simply stop saying your affirmation and just bring your attention back to your physical body. Slowly move your fingers and toes and gently open your eyes.

- ✓ **Mantra Meditation**

The mantra meditation is another very popular and powerful meditation technique. What is a mantra? A mantra is a sound, word, or syllable that acts as the point of focus in meditation. It helps to silence the mind as well as to evoke certain toes of energy. For this meditation, we are going to use the mantra, OM.

The mantra OM is very famous and powerful. It has been used by many spiritual masters and monks. It is also very common in Buddhism and Hinduism. It is believed that OM was also the very first sound in the universe. When you use the mantra OM, you do not just identify yourself with others who meditate, but you also tap the energy of many other spiritual masters and gurus in the world. Let us now move to the actual meditation proper:

Assume a meditative posture and relax. Now, start to say your mantra. In the beginning, you will have to say it out loud. However, after some time, the mantra will be a natural part of you that all you will need to do is close your eyes, and you will be able to hear it with your inner ear (clairaudience or clear hearing). This will happen once you get used to your mantra and have established a good connection to it. Keep your focus on your mantra. Relax and follow your mantra.

As you can see, this is a very simple technique, but it is also very powerful. This is why it has been a long time favorite among meditators, beginners as well as well-experienced ones.

If you are not comfortable with using the mantra OM, you are free to use other mantras. You can even come up with your own mantra.

However, when it comes to making your own mantra, you need to take note of some important points:

It has to be neutral

The mantra must not evoke an image or anything. For example, it is not good to use the word elephant as a mantra since it will make you imagine an elephant, which can cause your focus to be divided. Instead, choose a mantra that will not make you visualize anything so you can focus on it without a problem.

Easy to recite

You will have to say your mantra countless times, so be sure to use one that is easy to pronounce. It is also recommended to use a short mantra for convenience.

Use it many times

To establish a good connection with your mantra, you should use it many times. A good advice is to say your mantra even when you are not engaged in an actual meditation. For example, while driving or cooking. The point here is simply to get used to it and make it more a part of you. The more that you become closer to your mantra the more effective it will be. Just like with the use of affirmations, it is advised that you stick to using the same mantra. Hence, early in your spiritual journey, you are not encouraged to make time to try and choose the right mantra for you.

It is worth noting that a mantra does not need to mean anything. Its primary purpose is to help you still the mind by making the mind think of only a single thought (the mantra) instead of having too many thoughts (the monkey mind). Remember that your mantra should help you focus and still your mind.

✓ **White Light Meditation**

This is a good meditation technique especially if you want to trigger a lucid dream, also known as conscious dreaming. It is also a good way to just give you a relaxation as it will tend to make you fall asleep. The way to do this is as follows:

Close your eyes and relax. Consider everything that you see that is not black as light. Now, focus on the light. Be as relaxed as possible, even fall asleep, but keep your focus on the light. Let go.

What will happen here is that you will most likely start to see images after some time. These images will soon turn into a vision almost like a dream, but you will be conscious of it. Hence, you can take control of your dream. This exercise can even lead to an actual astral travel once you get good at it. Needless to say, it is not good to expect to see visions for reasons that we have already discussed. Instead, just focus on the light and let go.

Energy Charge

This is an excellent technique to get a boost of energy when you need it. This meditation technique fills your whole body with prana. Here are the instructions:

Assume a meditative posture and relax. Now, visualize a ray of white light descending from the sky and allow it to enter your crown chakra, and then into your body. Let it fill you with divine energy. See and feel your whole system filled with the strong current of energy from above. When you are satisfied and ready to end this exercise, simply see the ray of white light slowly fade away, and enjoy the boost of strong energy.

Another way to charge yourself with energy quickly, especially when you are feeling tired is by hugging a tree. As you hug it, feel its energy charging your system. Do not forget to thank the tree afterward.

Bubble Shield

This is a meditation technique that will allow you to create a protective shield around you to protect you from negative energies. If you deal with energies, then this is something that you should learn as you will be more sensitive to subtle energy, including negative energies. The steps are as follows:

Assume a meditative posture and relax. Visualize yourself surrounded by energy. For beginners, you can just see this energy as white light. Now, as you inhale, sea and feel that you draw energy from around you and have it form a bubble shield of protection around your body. With every inhalation, continue to charge your bubble shield. See and feel as it gets stronger and harder with every breath. Affirm, "This bubble shield protects me from all negative energies."

Take note that the strength of this bubble shield will dissipate over time. To keep your bubble shield strong, be sure to absorb more energy to replenish it. On average, a typical bubble shield can last for about five hours. The more that you are exposed to negative energy, the quicker that your bubble shield is going to weaken, so be sure to be sensitive enough about it. If you sense that it is getting weak, then replenish it with more energy. It is good to use this technique before you mingle with people or when you know that you are going to a place where you will be exposed to different kinds of energies, especially if it involves negative energy. It is also noteworthy that this shield gets stronger the more that you get used to it.

Alternate Nostril Breathing

This is a breathing technique that is used in yoga. When you use this technique, you will feel a sense of balance and tranquility. The way to do it is as follows:

Assume a meditative posture and relax. Try to keep a sense of balance by making your inhalation and exhalation of the same length duration. Relax and continue to focus on your breathing.

Although this may seem a very simple exercise, you might get surprised how effective and powerful it is. It will give you a sense of peace and mental balance, as well as clarity. It is not an excellent meditation technique both for beginners, as well as for experienced meditators. Be sure to give this a try.

Conclusion

Thank you for making it through to the end of Kundalini Awakening, let's hope it was informative and able to provide you with all of the tools you need to achieve your goals whatever they may be.

The next step is to continue your practice and see where your path leads. The exercises in this book are rooted in an ancient and mysterious past of Indian culture. They literally could be practiced for years without finding an end. Even the simplest meditation exercise can be practiced for decades without losing its potency and power. This shows the immense amount of potential that humans have to transform their lives and empower themselves that these practices have to offer.

The next step is to reaffirm every day that you are on your way to becoming a better, fuller you. Believe in yourself and your ability to make the changes necessary to realize your goals. Once you've removed the clutter from your mind, you will turn overthinking into focused achieving, each and every day. You may have heard many times over, "easier said than done." Well, you should be excited to learn how to do what you set your mind to do. You've wanted to make a change for a long time. Taking the steps to make your goals come to fruition is something many people never achieve.

It is times like this, after having taken a big step forward in my life, when I begin to reflect on how far I've come. It is hard to appreciate your progress sometimes when you are in the heat of battle and struggling every day during the beginning, middle, or even near the end of your efforts. There is nothing better than stepping up onto that final rung and looking down to see all of those completed steps in your wake.

Remember when you were sitting at square one, unable to free yourself from the chains of overthinking? I know it well—I've been there myself. It takes a great deal of courage to stand up and say, I'm ready to make a change. It saddens me to think that many people continue to overthink and overanalyze throughout their entire lives, missing out on the experiences and appreciation that a free mind can realize. It is easy to slip into the comfortable habits of mindless eating, checking a phone or tablet every few minutes, and going to bed later and later until your system is all out of sorts. Sometimes, it seems too easy to give in and let what's easy overshadow what's worth working for. You don't have to be a slave to overthinking, and maybe it's possible for you to take what you've learned and help change lives around you.

Perhaps you know someone who seems to be struggling with overthinking, stressing out about everyday challenges and stress just like you were at the beginning of your journey. Consider reaching out and sharing what you've learned. Nothing feels better than sharing new knowledge with someone who can use it to make the positive changes you've seen happen in yourself. Maybe it's a coworker, a spouse, or a close friend. Many people from different walks of life will benefit from the changes laid out in this book, so why not share your story!

THANK YOU FOR READING!

If you enjoyed this book, please consider leaving a review, even if it is only a line o two. It would make all the difference and would be very much appreciated.

Made in the USA
Las Vegas, NV
22 December 2021

39252423R00111